BASIC
HOME REPAIRS

By the Editors of Sunset Books

Sunset Books

Vice-President, General Manager: Richard A. Smeby
Vice-President, Editorial: Bob Doyle
Production Director: Lory Day
Art Director: Vasken Guiragossian

Basic Home Repairs was produced by
St. Remy Press
President: Pierre Léveillé
Managing Editor: Carolyn Jackson
Senior Editor: Heather Mills
Senior Art Director: Francine Lemieux
Editor: Alfred LeMaitre
Art Director: Solange Laberge
Assistant Editors: Caroline Bowden, Rebecca Smollett
Designers: François Daxhelet, Hélène Dion,
    Jean-Guy Doiron, François Longpré
Research Assistant: Adam van Sertima
Picture Editor: Christopher Jackson
Contributing Illustrators: Michel Blais, Jacques Perrault
Production Manager: Michelle Turbide
System Coordinator: Eric Beaulieu
Photographer: Robert Chartier
Proofreaders: Jane Pavanel, Veronica Schami,
    Elizabeth Warwick
Indexer: Christine M. Jacobs
Administrator: Natalie Watanabe
Other Staff: Normand Boudreault, Elizabeth Cameron,
    Lorraine Doré, Pierre Home-Douglas, Luc Germain

Book Consultant
Don Vandervort

Acknowledgments
Thanks to the following:
American Gas Association Laboratories, Cleveland, OH
René Bertrand, Blainville, Que.
Centre Do-It D'Agostino, Montreal, Que.
Richard Day, Palomar Mountain, CA
Delta Faucet Co., Indianapolis, IN
Gibson-Homans Co., Twinsburg, OH
Kenneth Larsen, C. Howard Simpkin Ltd., Montreal, Que.
Giles Miller-Mead, Brome, Que.
National Fire Protection Association, Quincy, MA
Niagara Mohawk Power Corporation, Syracuse, NY
Thomas Waterproof Coatings, Atlanta, GA
3M Canada Inc., London, Ont.
Underwriters' Laboratories, Melville, NY

Cover Credits:
Photographer: Noel Barnhurst
Cover concept and styling: Jean Warboy, Mary Ann Cleary

12 13 14 15 16 17 18 19 QPD QPD 02 01 00

ISBN 0-376-01581-0
Library of Congress Catalog Card Number: 94-069967
Printed in the United States

For more information on *Basic Home Repair* or any other
Sunset Book, call 1-800-526-5111 or see our website
at www.sunsetbooks.com.

CONTENTS

PREPARING FOR HOME REPAIRS

In this chapter, we'll take a quick look at the different kinds of emergencies that you're likely to encounter in your home, and offer the most effective solutions to deal with them.

You can prevent a costly or possibly tragic fire by following the suggestions found on page 5. This page also provides useful information on how to shut off the power supply during electrical emergencies. For homes that use gas-powered appliances, you'll find instructions on turning off the gas on page 7.

Plumbing crises can happen at any time—the most important thing to do is to shut off the water. Turn to page 8 for details.

The second part of this chapter shows the tools you'll encounter for home repairs. The shelves of a well-stocked hardware store or home improvement center display an impressive and sometimes bewildering range of tools, fasteners, and supplies. Throughout the book, we tell you exactly what tools are needed for each repair. In most cases, a range of general tools is sufficient—a selection is shown on pages 9 and 10. We also show some more specialized tools needed for repairs such as plumbing and electrical work. At the end of the chapter, we suggest basic supplies to keep on hand.

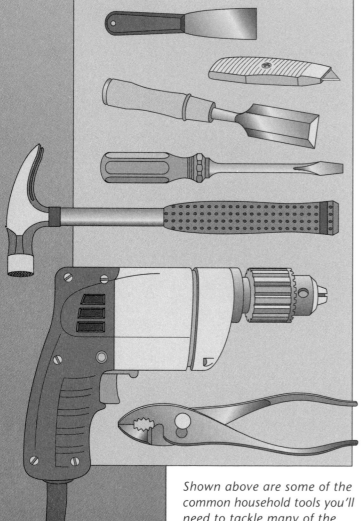

Shown above are some of the common household tools you'll need to tackle many of the repairs described in this book.

HOME EMERGENCIES

It's important to read this section, which deals with handling the most common household emergencies, before an emergency occurs. Be sure every member of your family knows and understands the steps to take in case of a fire, and familiarize everyone with the shutoff valves and switches that control the flow of water, electricity, and gas into your home. (If special wrenches are required to turn the valves, keep them close to the shutoffs.) Post emergency telephone numbers by each telephone.

In the event of a natural disaster such as an earthquake, flood, tornado, or hurricane, you may need to shut off the gas, electricity, and possibly the water. It's a good idea to have some basic emergency supplies—a portable radio, a flashlight with extra batteries, and a first aid kit with instructions for its use—on hand at all times.

Protect yourself and your family from fire danger by mapping out escape routes from your house, particularly from bedrooms, and have a central meeting area so everyone can be accounted for. Keep safety ladders near windows if your home is more than one story high. In the event of a fire in your home, get everyone out of the house and call the fire department from a neighbor's house.

Install one or more smoke detectors on every floor, near the exits, and adjacent to the bedrooms. Test the detectors once a month and replace the batteries when needed (usually once a year).

Equip your home with portable fire extinguishers and learn how to operate them before you need to use them. Extinguishers are classed by the type of fire they're designed to put out. If you have only one extinguisher, make sure it will extinguish all types of fires. Don't use water on an electrical fire.

For a small grease or oil fire in a pan, turn off the heat and cover the pan with a lid. Never pour water on a grease or oil fire—water will cause the fire to spread. In the case of an oven fire, turn off the heat and let the fire burn itself out. Don't open the oven door—this will let in more air, feeding the fire and causing it to continue to burn.

ELECTRICAL EMERGENCIES

Familiarize yourself with the information below before an emergency strikes. Be sure you know where the service entrance panel is and how to shut off the power in your type of disconnect. Keep a supply of fuses (if your system is equipped with them), as well as flashlights with extra batteries, and candles and matches. If the power fails suddenly, and the outage affects the neighborhood, notify the utility company. If the problem is just in your home, replace blown fuses or reset tripped circuit breakers *(page 48)*. If the outage recurs immediately, test for a short circuit or overload *(page 49)*.

If an appliance begins to smoke, spark, or catch fire, unplug it (if the plug is sparking, pull it out by the cord) or shut it off at the wall switch. Don't touch the appliance itself. If you can't unplug the appliance or if it doesn't have a wall switch to shut off, turn off the power to the circuit. When the appliance cools, take it to a repair shop or call a service representative.

The following pages show you how to shut off the main power supply, shut off power to a circuit, remove a plug fuse, and trip a circuit breaker. NOTE: Water and electricity don't mix. Protect yourself from shock if the floor is damp by working with one hand and wearing thick rubber gloves, by standing on a dry piece of wood, or wearing dry rubber boots. If the floor is flooded, don't try to throw a circuit breaker; instead, call your utility. Finally, you should also know how to turn the power back on once it's safe.

Shutting off the main power supply

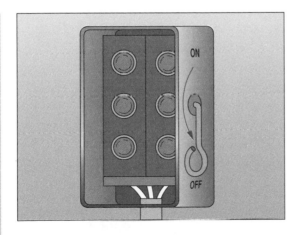

Shutting off a lever disconnect
If your home has this type of fused service entrance panel, you can shut off the power to your entire electrical system at the lever disconnect *(left)*. The panel may be located on the exterior of your home below the electric meter or on an inside wall directly behind the meter. When you pull the external handle of the lever disconnect to the OFF position, the main power supply is shut off.

Disconnecting a pull-out block

Pull firmly on the non-metallic pull-out blocks *(right)* to remove them from the cabinet. This will disconnect the power supply.

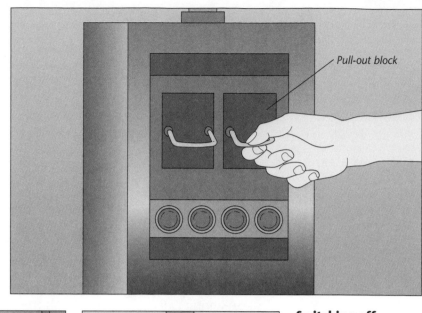

Pull-out block

Disconnecting a single main circuit breaker

Switch the main breaker *(below)* to OFF to cut the power supply.

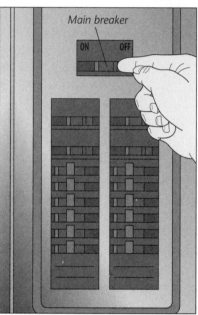

Main breaker

ON   OFF

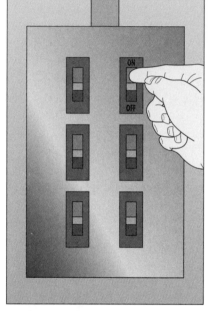

ON

OFF

Switching off multiple main circuit breakers

All of the breakers in the main section *(left)* must be switched to the OFF position to disconnect the power.

Shutting off power to a circuit

TOOLKIT
• Fuse puller (optional)

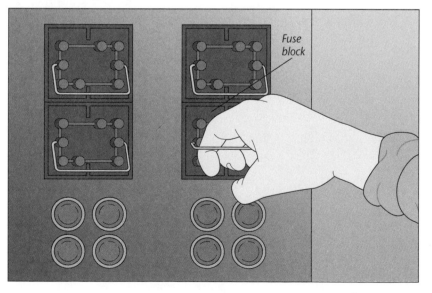

Fuse block

Removing a cartridge fuse

Find the fuse block that protects the circuit you wish to shut off. Grasping the handle firmly, pull out the fuse block *(left)*. Release the cartridge fuse from the spring clips either by hand or by using a fuse puller.

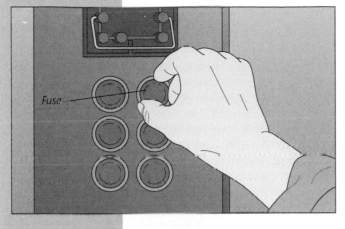

Removing a plug fuse
In the service panel, locate the plug fuse controlling the circuit you will be working on. Grasp the fuse by its insulated rim and unscrew it *(left)*. Check that electrical devices on the circuit are dead. If not, repeat the procedure until you find the right fuse.

Tripping a circuit breaker
Find the circuit breaker protecting the circuit to be shut off, then push the toggle to the OFF position. To reset, simply flip the toggle to the ON position *(right)*. The procedure for resetting a circuit breaker varies, but instructions will often be on the breaker. Many modern circuit breakers go to an intermediate position when they trip. To reset, push the toggle firmly to OFF before returning to ON.

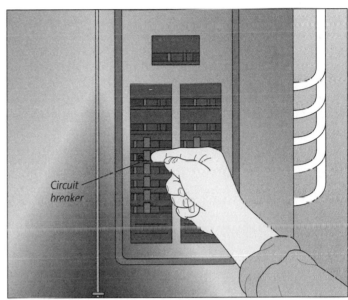

GAS LEAKS

If you ever smell gas anywhere in your house, you should take the following precautions: First, get everyone outside the house immediately; open as many windows and doors as possible to help clear the gas from the house. Call your gas company or the fire department from a neighbor's house. Don't light a match and don't turn on any electrical switch—the danger of fire or explosion is severe.

In the event of a natural disaster, such as an earthquake, flood, tornado, or hurricane, or if you have a severe leak inside that you've not been able to stop, you may have to turn off the gas supply yourself. Make sure that you and all the members of your family know the location of the gas shutoff valve and how to operate it. It's a good idea to keep a specially labeled adjustable wrench close at hand in the event of an emergency.

Turning off the gas

TOOLKIT
• Adjustable wrench

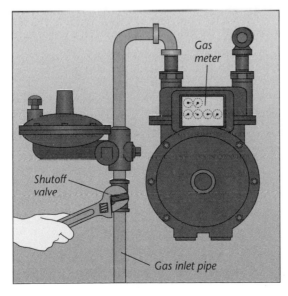

Working the gas shutoff valve
Once everyone's out of the house, you can turn off the main gas supply at the gas shutoff valve (or wait for the utility company to do it). The valve is located on the gas inlet pipe next to the gas meter. To shut off the valve, use an adjustable wrench to turn it a quarter turn (in either direction) so the valve is perpendicular to the pipe. Don't turn the gas back on until you've found the source of the problem and corrected it.

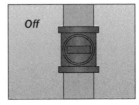

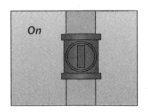

PLUMBING EMERGENCIES

In a plumbing emergency, you'll need to stop the flow of water quickly. To do this, you and your family need to know the location of the shutoff valve for every fixture and appliance, as well as the main shutoff valve for the house, and how they operate. To learn about your plumbing system and how it works, turn to page 32.

For a leaking or broken pipe, turn off the main shutoff valve to prevent water damage and make temporary repairs to stop the leak *(page 47)*; the pipe will have to be replaced as soon as it's convenient to do so.

When you have to deal with an overflowing toilet bowl, reach inside the toilet tank, push the tank stopper down into the valve seat, and hold it there *(page 45)*.

Turn off the water at the fixture shutoff valve underneath the toilet. If there's no valve there, turn off the house shutoff valve. Then, unclog the toilet using a toilet plunger or toilet auger *(page 34)*.

If your sink is clogged, shut off any faucet or appliance (such as a dishwasher) that's draining into it. Unclog the sink using a sink plunger or drain-and-trap auger *(page 33)*. Don't use a chemical drain cleaner if the blockage is total.

If you have a faucet that won't shut off, immediately turn off the water at the fixture shutoff valve underneath the sink. If there's no valve there, turn off the house shutoff valve. Repair the faucet *(page 36)* or, if necessary, replace it.

Shutting off the water

TOOLKIT
• Wrench (optional)

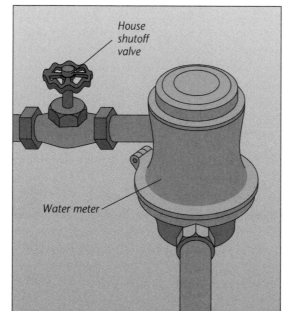

House shutoff valve

Water meter

Using the house shutoff valve
If the problem is not with a particular fixture or appliance or if there's no shutoff valve for the fixture or appliance, use the house shutoff valve *(left)* to turn off the entire water supply to your home. You'll find the house shutoff valve on the inside or outside of your house where the main water supply pipe enters. (In cold climates, look just inside the foundation wall in the basement or crawl space.) Turn the valve clockwise to shut it off. If you need a wrench to turn the valve, keep one, specially labeled, near the valve.

If the house shutoff valve itself is defective, call your water utility so they can send someone out to shut off the water before it reaches the valve.

Using the fixture shutoff valve
If the emergency involves a specific fixture or appliance, first look for its shutoff valve and turn it clockwise to shut off the water to that fixture or appliance only. The valve *(right)* is usually located underneath a fixture such as a sink or a toilet, or behind an appliance, such as a clothes washer, at the point where the water supply pipe (or pipes) connects to it.

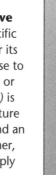

Fixture shutoff valve

TOOLS OF THE TRADE

The standard tools pictured are useful for a variety of home repairs. You may want to purchase a number of these tools in advance, or equip your workshop as the need arises. When you do buy a tool, buy the best you can afford; quality tools make the job easier and are safer than bargain-basement varieties. The specialty tools shown on pages 10 and 11 are needed for specific repairs shown in this book; buy them as needed.

It's a good idea to keep your workshop stocked with the supplies listed on page 11. Some, such as sandpaper, are needed for a number of different types of repairs; others, such as epoxy putty for patching pipes, are good to have on hand for emergencies. Other supplies needed for a specific job are listed with the repair instructions.

In addition to the basic tools and supplies described in the following pages, you should also be prepared with basic safety equipment:
• Safety goggles or glasses: Wear when using any striking tool and when working with a material that could splash, such as mortar.
• Work gloves: Wear when working with sharp or rough materials.
• Rubber gloves: Wear when working with caustic products or household waste.
• Dust mask: Wear when working with dusty materials, such as when sanding.
• Respirator: Wear when using products such as adhesives or paints that give off toxic fumes.

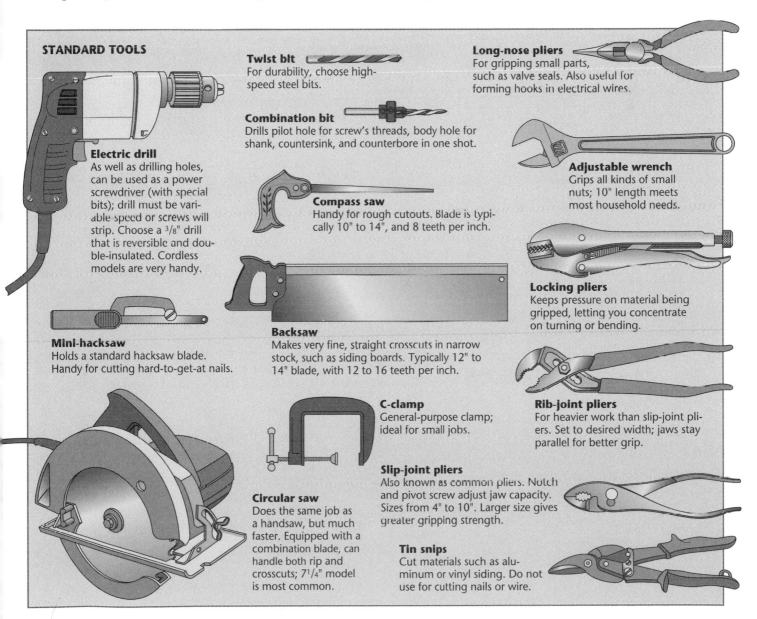

STANDARD TOOLS

Electric drill
As well as drilling holes, can be used as a power screwdriver (with special bits); drill must be variable-speed or screws will strip. Choose a 3/8" drill that is reversible and double-insulated. Cordless models are very handy.

Twist bit
For durability, choose high-speed steel bits.

Combination bit
Drills pilot hole for screw's threads, body hole for shank, countersink, and counterbore in one shot.

Compass saw
Handy for rough cutouts. Blade is typically 10" to 14", and 8 teeth per inch.

Long-nose pliers
For gripping small parts, such as valve seals. Also useful for forming hooks in electrical wires.

Adjustable wrench
Grips all kinds of small nuts; 10" length meets most household needs.

Locking pliers
Keeps pressure on material being gripped, letting you concentrate on turning or bending.

Mini-hacksaw
Holds a standard hacksaw blade. Handy for cutting hard-to-get-at nails.

Backsaw
Makes very fine, straight crosscuts in narrow stock, such as siding boards. Typically 12" to 14" blade, with 12 to 16 teeth per inch.

C-clamp
General-purpose clamp; ideal for small jobs.

Rib-joint pliers
For heavier work than slip-joint pliers. Set to desired width; jaws stay parallel for better grip.

Slip-joint pliers
Also known as common pliers. Notch and pivot screw adjust jaw capacity. Sizes from 4" to 10". Larger size gives greater gripping strength.

Circular saw
Does the same job as a handsaw, but much faster. Equipped with a combination blade, can handle both rip and crosscuts; 7 1/4" model is most common.

Tin snips
Cut materials such as aluminum or vinyl siding. Do not use for cutting nails or wire.

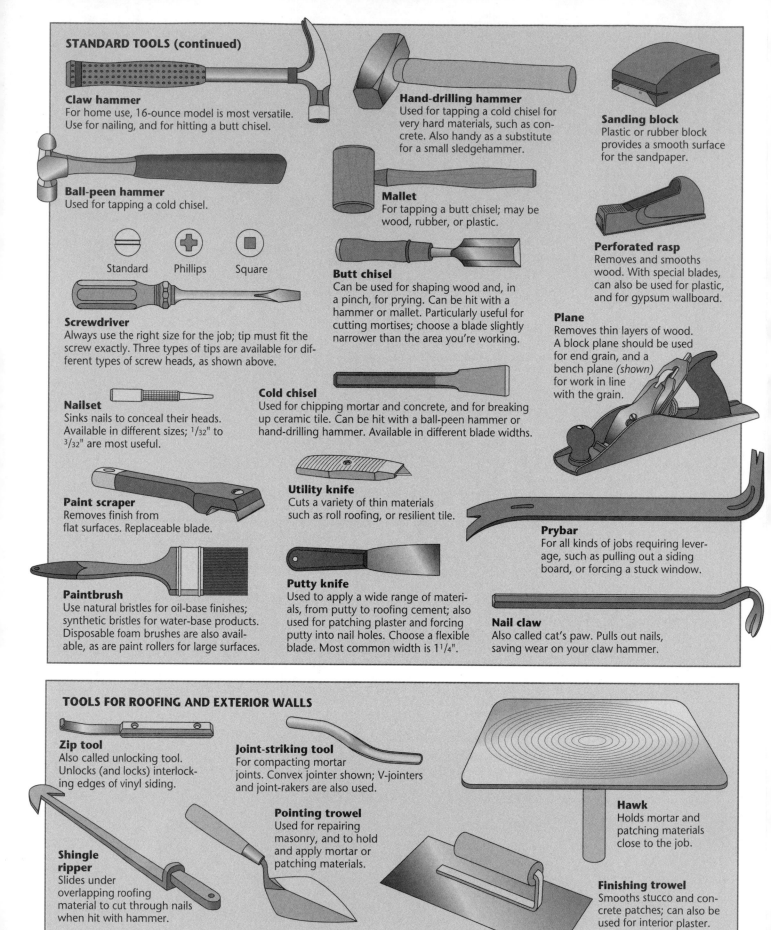

STANDARD TOOLS (continued)

Claw hammer
For home use, 16-ounce model is most versatile. Use for nailing, and for hitting a butt chisel.

Ball-peen hammer
Used for tapping a cold chisel.

Standard   Phillips   Square

Screwdriver
Always use the right size for the job; tip must fit the screw exactly. Three types of tips are available for different types of screw heads, as shown above.

Nailset
Sinks nails to conceal their heads. Available in different sizes; 1/32" to 3/32" are most useful.

Paint scraper
Removes finish from flat surfaces. Replaceable blade.

Paintbrush
Use natural bristles for oil-base finishes; synthetic bristles for water-base products. Disposable foam brushes are also available, as are paint rollers for large surfaces.

Hand-drilling hammer
Used for tapping a cold chisel for very hard materials, such as concrete. Also handy as a substitute for a small sledgehammer.

Mallet
For tapping a butt chisel; may be wood, rubber, or plastic.

Butt chisel
Can be used for shaping wood and, in a pinch, for prying. Can be hit with a hammer or mallet. Particularly useful for cutting mortises; choose a blade slightly narrower than the area you're working.

Cold chisel
Used for chipping mortar and concrete, and for breaking up ceramic tile. Can be hit with a ball-peen hammer or hand-drilling hammer. Available in different blade widths.

Utility knife
Cuts a variety of thin materials such as roll roofing, or resilient tile.

Putty knife
Used to apply a wide range of materials, from putty to roofing cement; also used for patching plaster and forcing putty into nail holes. Choose a flexible blade. Most common width is 1 1/4".

Sanding block
Plastic or rubber block provides a smooth surface for the sandpaper.

Perforated rasp
Removes and smooths wood. With special blades, can also be used for plastic, and for gypsum wallboard.

Plane
Removes thin layers of wood. A block plane should be used for end grain, and a bench plane (shown) for work in line with the grain.

Prybar
For all kinds of jobs requiring leverage, such as pulling out a siding board, or forcing a stuck window.

Nail claw
Also called cat's paw. Pulls out nails, saving wear on your claw hammer.

TOOLS FOR ROOFING AND EXTERIOR WALLS

Zip tool
Also called unlocking tool. Unlocks (and locks) interlocking edges of vinyl siding.

Joint-striking tool
For compacting mortar joints. Convex jointer shown; V-jointers and joint-rakers are also used.

Pointing trowel
Used for repairing masonry, and to hold and apply mortar or patching materials.

Shingle ripper
Slides under overlapping roofing material to cut through nails when hit with hammer.

Hawk
Holds mortar and patching materials close to the job.

Finishing trowel
Smooths stucco and concrete patches; can also be used for interior plaster.

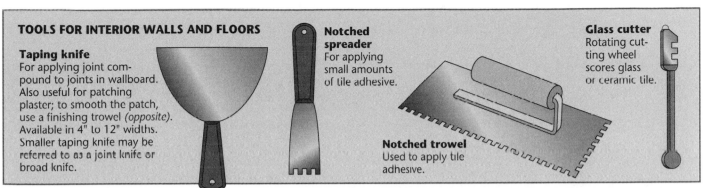

TOOLS FOR INTERIOR WALLS AND FLOORS

Taping knife
For applying joint compound to joints in wallboard. Also useful for patching plaster; to smooth the patch, use a finishing trowel *(opposite)*. Available in 4" to 12" widths. Smaller taping knife may be referred to as a joint knife or broad knife.

Notched spreader
For applying small amounts of tile adhesive.

Notched trowel
Used to apply tile adhesive.

Glass cutter
Rotating cutting wheel scores glass or ceramic tile.

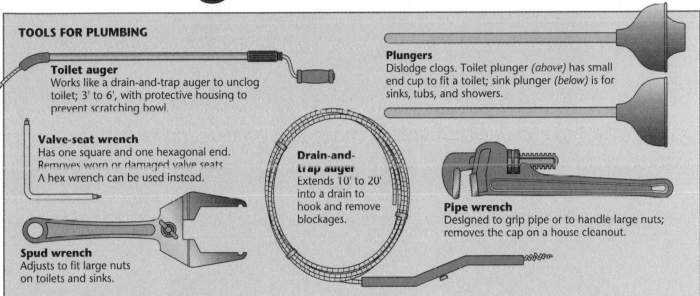

TOOLS FOR PLUMBING

Toilet auger
Works like a drain-and-trap auger to unclog toilet; 3' to 6', with protective housing to prevent scratching bowl.

Valve-seat wrench
Has one square and one hexagonal end. Removes worn or damaged valve seats. A hex wrench can be used instead.

Spud wrench
Adjusts to fit large nuts on toilets and sinks.

Drain-and-trap auger
Extends 10' to 20' into a drain to hook and remove blockages.

Plungers
Dislodge clogs. Toilet plunger *(above)* has small end cup to fit a toilet; sink plunger *(below)* is for sinks, tubs, and showers.

Pipe wrench
Designed to grip pipe or to handle large nuts; removes the cap on a house cleanout.

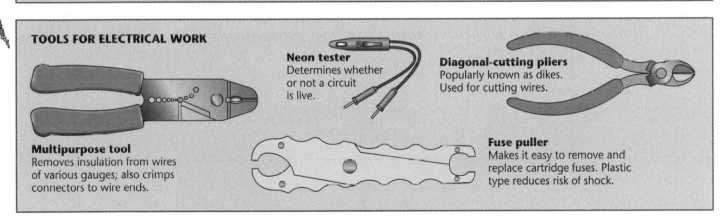

TOOLS FOR ELECTRICAL WORK

Neon tester
Determines whether or not a circuit is live.

Diagonal-cutting pliers
Popularly known as dikes. Used for cutting wires.

Multipurpose tool
Removes insulation from wires of various gauges; also crimps connectors to wire ends.

Fuse puller
Makes it easy to remove and replace cartridge fuses. Plastic type reduces risk of shock.

HANDY HOME-REPAIR SUPPLIES

- Sandpaper: Keep a variety of grits; a larger number is a finer grit. You'll need wet-or-dry type for wet sanding.
- Steel wool: 00 is a good multipurpose grade.
- Roof patch: For emergency repair of leaks.
- Glue: An all-purpose wood glue is a good choice.
- Epoxy putty: For patching pipes.
- Fasteners: A range of nails, screws, and washers.
- Fuses: Exact replacements for those in your home.

- Powdered graphite: To lubricate locks and sliding doors.
- Light penetrating oil: For lubricating bearings, rollers, door handles, etc., and for freeing plumbing connections.
- Faucet washers: Keep a range if you have compression faucets.
- Bicycle inner-tube: For patching pipes.
- Hose clamps: For patching pipes.
- Silicone caulk (and caulking gun): For stopping drafts, sealing tubs, etc.

OUTDOOR REPAIRS

The house cladding—its exterior walls and roof—is what keeps the weather out. In order to ensure that it continues to do so, inspect the outside of your house regularly to fix any damage before it becomes more serious; ultimately, the structure of your house could be compromised.

In this chapter, you'll learn how to undertake common repairs to various types of siding and roofing. The section on the different types of siding—wood, plywood and hardboard sheets, aluminum, and vinyl—begins on the opposite page. Paint problems and solutions are discussed on page 16. The next section, beginning on page 18, explains how to repair masonry walls.

In the section on roofing repairs *(page 22)*, we first show you how to locate a roof leak, and how to fix gutters. Regular maintenance of your gutter-and-downspout system is important to keep water flowing freely off your roof. Finally, we show you how to repair flashings, and the roofing materials themselves—asphalt shingles, wood shingles and shakes, masonry and metal roof tiles, and built-up or roll roofing.

Whenever you're working up high, either on upper parts of siding, or on your roof, always be extremely careful; consider setting up scaffolding. If you have a steep roof, call in a professional to do a roofing job.

Turn to the chapter on indoor repairs for doors *(page 75)* and windows *(page 88)*.

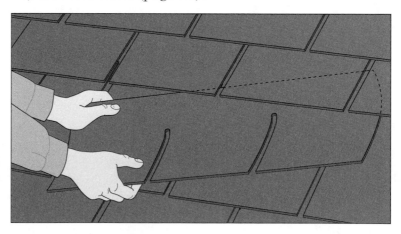

Replace damaged shingles before the roof starts to leak. Inspect your roof regularly for wear.

SIDING

Siding is made from various materials, each of which requires a specific repair technique. This section covers siding made of solid wood boards, plywood or hardboard panels, and aluminum or vinyl.

Plywood and hardboard panel sidings are repaired differently than wood board sidings because of both their makeup and their size. Aluminum and vinyl siding can become dented and scratched over the course of its lifetime. These can be fixed without having to replace the siding; however, more extensive damage will require new siding.

If you have wood shingles or shakes on your walls, replace any that are damaged (split, curled, warped, or broken). The technique for this depends on whether they are applied in single or double courses (rows): In a single-course application, where each course overlaps the one below, follow the instructions on page 26 for a roof shingle or shake. Double-coursing, with two complete layers of shingles or shakes, has exposed nailheads. To replace a damaged shingle or shake, pull out the nails, remove the damaged piece, slide in a replacement, and nail it on.

WOOD BOARD SIDING

Wood board siding is durable, but needs regular maintenance. To prevent deterioration, repair simple surface problems as soon as possible—fill holes in the wood, fix warped and split boards, and repaint. Boards that are badly damaged should be replaced (page 14), but determine the cause of any serious damage first. Moisture may be the culprit; try to find the source by checking for deteriorating roofing (page 22), leaking gutters or downspouts, (page 23) or poor drainage. Consult a professional if you can't locate the source, or if you see evidence of dry rot or insect infestation. Once you pinpoint the problem, make the necessary repairs immediately; new siding installed over problem areas will just deteriorate again after a short time.

Minor repairs are easy to do. Fill a small hole with wood putty (available in a variety of shades for matching stained wood) and allow it to dry completely. If the hole is fairly large, apply the putty in layers, letting each one dry completely before applying the next. When the final layer is dry, sand the surface smooth, and if necessary finish the putty to match the surrounding siding.

Sometimes, a board is so badly damaged or decayed that your only choice is to replace it. The approach to replacing board siding depends on the milling of the boards and how they're nailed. You'll have to cut the

damaged piece and remove the nails in order to pry it out; for overlapping styles of siding, such as clapboard, you may need to pry up the board above the one you're replacing to free the last pieces of damaged board. After repairing any damage to the building paper with roofing cement, carefully measure and cut the new piece—which must match the original—so it will fit correctly. For best results, cut out and replace a section that spans at least three studs (use a carpenter's square to mark cutting lines at right angles, and centered over the studs). Pull nails out of the old siding with a nail claw, or cut off nails from behind siding with a mini-hacksaw.

For board-and-batten siding, pry up the battens on either side of the damaged board far enough to raise the nailheads, then pull out the nails to remove the damaged board. Patch any cuts in the building paper with roofing cement. Replace the damaged board and batten with identically sized new ones. Caulk all joints, then stain or paint.

Paint problems (page 16) can have a variety of causes: wrong paint, improper surface preparation, careless painting, long-term exposure to harsh sunlight, or improper wall ventilation (consider adding vents to the roof, gables, and soffits, or installing a fan). Usually the problem can be remedied with a proper paint job.

Repairing a warped board	**Fastening the board**

Fastening the board

Boards that have been fitted too tightly during installation will tend to warp or buckle when they swell with moisture. To straighten such a board, first try to pull it into line by driving long screws through it and into the wall studs: Drill countersunk holes (page 73), then insert the screws and tighten them. Cover the holes with wood putty, then sand and finish the area.

If that doesn't work, you can shorten the board to give it more room. Use a mini-hacksaw to cut the nails within the warped area, and continue removing nails to the nearest end of the board. Pull out the end of the board, then use a rasp, sander, or block plane to remove wood on the end, little by little, until the board fits. Renail the board.

Repairing a split board

TOOLKIT
- Butt chisel
- Hammer or screwdriver
- Putty knife, sanding block, and paint-brush (optional)

1 ▶ Gluing the split
A clean split or crack can be repaired by carefully prying the board apart with a chisel, then coating both edges with waterproof glue *(right)*.

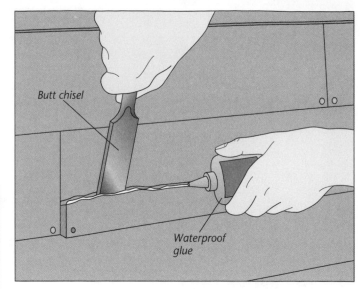

Butt chisel

Waterproof glue

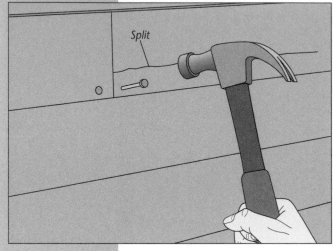

Split

◀ 2 Fastening the board
Push the edges of the two pieces tightly together, drill holes and secure both sections to the sheathing with nails or screws *(left)*. Fill any gaps around the split with putty, then sand and finish to match the rest of the board.

Replacing a damaged tongue-and-groove board

TOOLKIT
- Nail claw
- Circular saw
- Chisel and mallet
- Hammer
- Putty knife
- Sanding block
- Paintbrush

1 ▶ Removing the board
Because the boards are locked together by the tongues and grooves, the damaged piece must be split lengthwise as well as cut at the ends before it can be removed. (Shiplap and channel rustic siding are also replaced this way.) Pull out all exposed nails in the area to be re-moved. Mark the end-cut lines, then make cuts with a circular saw almost to the top and bottom of each mark; set the blade depth just shy of the thick-ness of the siding. Hold the blade guard back and plunge the moving blade down into the wood to start each cut; finish the cuts with a chisel and mallet. Rip along the center of the damaged section, cutting almost to the end cuts *(right, above)*. Hold the saw firmly—it may kick back. Also, be careful not to cut into adjacent boards. Cave in the board; then pull out the loosened pieces *(right, below)*. Repair any cuts in the building paper with roofing cement (applied with a putty knife).

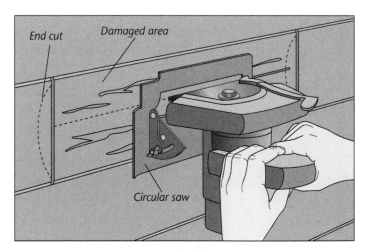

End cut   Damaged area

Circular saw

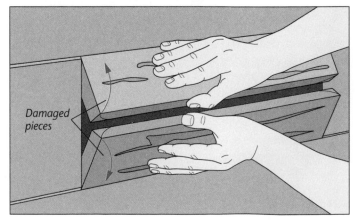

Damaged pieces

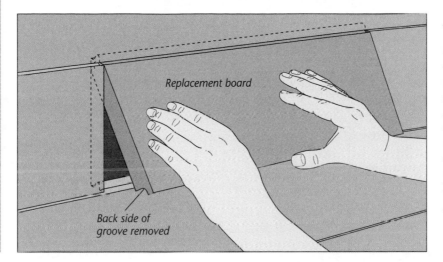

2 **Installing a new board**

Remove the back side of the groove on the replacement board; slide it in place (*left*) and face-nail the board. Countersink the nail-heads, caulk or putty the nail holes and end joints, sand, and finish the board to match the others.

Replacement board

Back side of groove removed

Repairing a damaged clapboard siding board

TOOLKIT
- Backsaw
- Prybar
- Compass saw or chisel
- Mini-hacksaw or nail claw
- Hammer
- Putty knife
- Caulking gun (optional)
- Sanding block
- Paintbrush

1 **Removing the board**

Mark cutting lines on each side of the damaged area. To provide a solid nailing base for the replacement board, center the lines over wall studs. You can use a backsaw to cut clapboard and other overlapped types of siding, such as bevel and Dolly Varden. Pull out any nails in the way of your saw cuts. Pry up the bottom edge of the damaged board with a prybar. Drive small wooden wedges underneath the board at either end outside the cutting lines to keep it raised. Cut through the board along both cutting lines; finish the cuts with a compass saw or a chisel. Break the damaged board out—in pieces, if necessary. Cut any nails passing through the board above with a mini-hacksaw (*inset*)—or pull them out—to free the top of the damaged board. Repair any tears in the building paper with roofing cement.

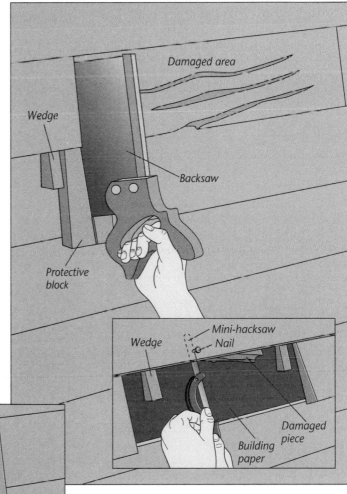

Damaged area

Wedge

Backsaw

Protective block

Wedge

Mini-hacksaw

Nail

Building paper

Damaged piece

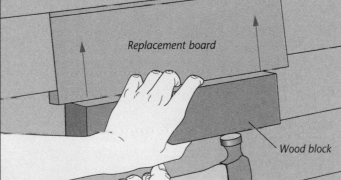

Replacement board

Wood block

2 **Installing a new board**

Trim the replacement board to length and drive it into position by hammering against a wood block (*left*). Nail along its bottom edge, into the sheathing. Caulk or putty the nail holes and board ends; sand, then stain or paint the new board to match the existing siding.

Paint damage on exterior wood surfaces can result from any number of causes. Before you repaint, try to diagnose the cause of the problem so it won't happen again. Then you can prepare the surface, select an appropriate paint or stain, and apply the finish, as explained below.

Typical causes of paint damage include improper surface preparation, careless painting, use of the wrong paint, and structural problems that trap moisture in the wood (sometimes walls need a vapor barrier). **Blistering** occurs when water or solvent vapor is trapped under the paint. Cut the blister open: If you find bare wood underneath, it's a water blister created by moisture escaping from damp wood. If you find paint, it's a solvent blister, often caused by painting in direct sunlight or on wet wood. **Peeling** happens when paint is applied over dirty, greasy, or wet wood, or over loose paint. **Alligatoring**, a checkered pattern of cracks resembling alligator skin results when the top coat is applied before the bottom coat is dry or when the bottom and top coat paints are incompatible. **Wrinkling** will result if paint is applied too thickly; the top surface dries too rapidly and the paint underneath droops down. Although high-quality exterior paint is designed to chalk so rain will clean dirt from the surface, **chalking** that comes off when you rub up against the surface indicates that the surface was unprimed or finished with paint of poor quality.

Wood surfaces must be clean, dry, and in good condition before you repaint. Repair any damaged boards, trim, or shingles and if there is any structural damage that allows water to penetrate, get it fixed. Remove dirt and all loose, peeling, or blistering paint with a stiff wire brush or paint scraper. Where paint damage is severe, remove the paint down to the bare wood. Feather the edges of any remaining sound paint with medium-grade sandpaper, then sand again with fine-grade sandpaper. If the top coat didn't adhere to a previous coat, rough up the damaged paint with sandpaper. Wash greasy or very dirty wood with a mild detergent, hose it off, and let the wood dry before painting.

For moisture problems, apply a water repellent, then a prime coat, and cover with two coats of high-quality paint after you've prepared the surface.

Apply a clear waterproofing sealer to the ends of all wood boards to prevent water penetration. Brush a prime coat on bare or new wood. Where heat and humidity cause wood to deteriorate quickly, treat boards with a wood preservative before sealing.

Protect wood by painting or staining it (the exceptions are redwood, cedar, and southern red cypress—which need only to be sealed to help retard color changes). Use a finish that matches the existing one as closely as possible. Use a 2-inch brush for trim and a 4-inch brush for wider surfaces. For a larger area, you may want to use a 9-inch roller; choose a fine nap for smooth surfaces and a thick nap for textured surfaces.

Paint exteriors in fair, dry weather with temperatures between 50° and 90°F. Wait until the morning dew has evaporated and stop before evening dampness sets in.

PLYWOOD AND HARDBOARD SIDING

Damage to a small area of plywood or hardboard panels can be repaired by replacing a piece, as shown below; instructions for other minor repairs are found opposite.

If a panel has extensive damage, it will have to be replaced. Many problems are caused by exposure to the elements; make sure to maintain the finish on your siding.

Repairing a damaged panel

TOOLKIT
- Carpenter's square
- Circular saw
- Handsaw
- Putty knife (optional)
- Hammer
- Caulking gun
- Paintbrush

Replacing a damaged section
Mark the cuts to be made using a square for accuracy; center vertical cuts over studs. Remove the damaged section with a circular saw *(right)*; use a handsaw at the corners. Install 2x4 backing where needed to support edges of the replacement piece. Cut the replacement to fit, repair any tears in the building paper with roofing cement, and nail the new piece in place. Caulk the nailheads and seams, then finish the patch to match the rest of the panel.

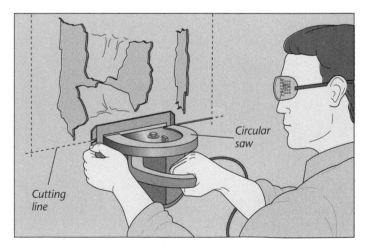
Circular saw
Cutting line

Making minor repairs to panels

Fixing a panel
Repair checks in plywood (small splits in the surface veneer) by sanding them down and filling with wood putty or a flexible, all-purpose filler. Sand again, then refinish to match existing siding. If a panel edge is delaminating (the layers are separating), apply waterproof glue between plies and then nail them down.

For hardboard siding, fill small holes with filler, then sand and paint. For a deeper hole, build the patch up, filling 2 or 3 times before sanding. If the panel is buckling, and the finish is intact, check the nailing: The siding should be fastened with properly spaced box nails that are long enough to penetrate studs at least 1 1/2".

ALUMINUM AND VINYL SIDING

Aluminum and vinyl siding panels with serious damage must be replaced, as shown below. Each piece has interlocking flanges along its edges, and is nailed to the sheathing through slots along one flange; the other flange interlocks with the adjacent panel.

Minor repairs can be made to aluminum siding: Remove corrosion with fine steel wool, then apply metal primer and latex paint. Use the same painting technique to conceal scratches. To remove a dent, drill a hole in its center and drive in a self-tapping screw with two washers under the screw head. Gently pull on the screw head with pliers. Remove the screw and fill the hole with aluminum filler, following label directions. When dry, sand smooth and touch up with matching paint.

Replacing aluminum siding

TOOLKIT
• Utility knife
• Straightedge
• Tin snips

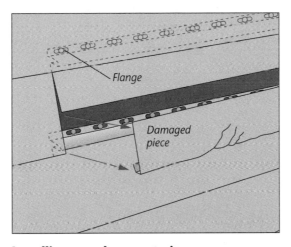 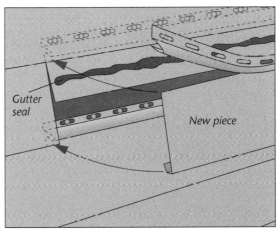

Installing a replacement piece
Cut through the center of the panel to just beyond both sides of the damaged area, using a utility knife. Make vertical cuts at both ends; remove the lower part of the damaged section, leaving the rest of the panel in place (above, left). Cut the nailing strip off the replacement by scoring it with a utility knife and snapping it off, then use tin snips to cut this piece so it overlaps the existing siding by 3" on each side. Apply butyl gutter seal along the nailing strip and press the new piece into place (above, right), hooking the base into the interlocking edge of the section below. Hold or prop until dry.

Replacing vinyl siding

TOOLKIT
• Zip tool
• Carpenter's square
• Tin snips or backsaw
• Hammer

Installing a replacement piece
Try to work in warm weather, when the vinyl is pliable. Use a zip tool to undo the panel next to or above the damaged one; bend it out carefully and remove the nails holding the damaged piece. Mark cutting lines on each side of the damaged area; use a carpenter's square for accuracy. With tin snips or a backsaw, cut the panel along the lines and remove the damaged section. Cut a replacement piece, allowing for a 1" overlap at each end (or at one end if the damaged section ends at a corner or joint). Snap the top edge of the new section in place and nail it with aluminum or galvanized box nails that are long enough to penetrate at least 1" into the sheathing. Use the zip tool to hook the upper panel over the new panel's lock.

MASONRY WALLS

Most problems with brick or stone veneer develop at the mortar joints. The mortar can shrink causing the joints to open, or if it contains lime, the mortar can crumble. Freeze-thaw cycles in cold climates, excess moisture, and settling can break down the mortar. To ensure strong, watertight joints, you'll have to remove the cracked or crumbling mortar and repoint the joints, which means filling them with new mortar.

Cracks up to 1/8 inch in a concrete foundation wall are common and are not usually cause for concern; hairline cracks and slightly wider cracks can be patched as explained opposite. However, if the crack is wider than 1/8 inch, or if its edges aren't parallel, it may indicate a structural problem. These cracks, as well as cracks that cause leaking should be inspected by a professional.

Because stucco is a rigid material, it cracks if a house moves with settling or earthquakes. It's also susceptible to moisture damage if it isn't applied properly. Whether or not to repair your own stucco is a tough call. The chances are good that you can handle minor repairs successfully; but if problem areas are fairly extensive, it may be wise to have a professional do the work. Most important to a good repair job are slow curing of the stucco and careful matching of color and texture to the existing wall.

Repointing damaged mortar joints

TOOLKIT
- Cold chisel
- Ball-peen hammer
- Pointing trowel or joint filler
- Hawk
- Joint-striking tool or steel rod
- Stiff brush or broom

1 ▶ **Removing damaged mortar**
Fresh mortar will not adhere to old very well. Chisel out the cracked and crumbling old mortar with a narrow-blade cold chisel and a ball-peen hammer *(right)*, exposing as much of the mortar-bearing faces of the units as possible. Expose the joints to a depth of at least 3/4", then thoroughly brush and blow them out, using an old paintbrush.

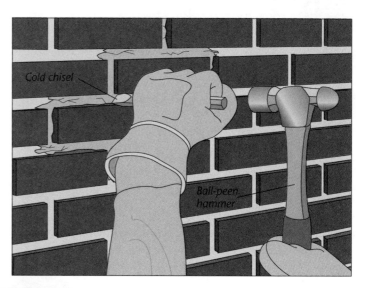

Cold chisel
Ball-peen hammer

Pointing trowel
Mortar
Hawk

2 ◀ **Filling the joints**
First, dampen the area. Although you can make your own mortar, it's easier to use dry packaged mortar available at building supply stores. Use weather-resistant type N and follow package directions, mixing a stiff mortar. (If you're repairing stone, mix mortar without lime—1 part portland cement to 3 or 4 parts masonry sand.) When the units are still damp, but not shiny wet, use a joint filler or small pointing trowel *(left)* to fill the joints completely. A hawk will help you hold the mortar. Mortar is caustic, so wear work gloves.

 PLAY IT SAFE

PROTECT YOUR EYES
When you chip out old mortar with a ball-peen hammer and cold chisel, bits of mortar can fly out. Always protect your eyes with safety goggles or glasses.

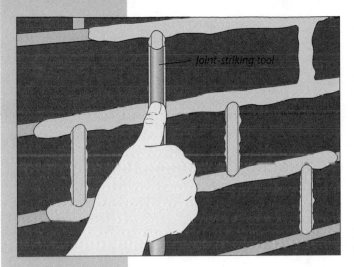
Joint-striking tool

3 Tooling the joints

When the mortar is just stiff enough to retain a thumb print, the joints should be tooled, or "struck." Striking the joints compresses the mortar, waterproofing the joints and contributing to the strength of the wall. Use a special joint-striking tool, a steel rod, or the pointing trowel to tool the joints to match the existing joints. Draw the tool along the vertical joints first *(left)*, and then along the horizontal ones.

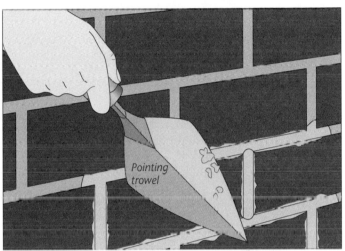
Pointing trowel

4 Cleaning up the joints

Cut off any tags (excess mortar) by sliding a trowel along the wall *(right)*. Then restrike the joints as in the previous step. When the mortar is well set, brush the wall with a stiff brush or broom. Keep the joints damp for about four days so the mortar can fully cure.

Patching a small crack in concrete

TOOLKIT
- Stiff brush
- Paintbrush (optional)
- Putty knife

Filling the crack

First brush the dirt out of the crack using a stiff brush. You'll need latex concrete patching compound to fill the crack. Some products may also require a bonding agent, which can be applied with a paintbrush—check the directions. Fill the crack with patching compound, using a putty knife; apply a little more compound than the crack will hold. Then, go back with the putty knife to scrape off excess compound. Dampen the patch with a light mist of water when the edges start to look dry, and then cover it with plastic and let it cure for the number of days recommended by the manufacturer.

Patching a wide crack in concrete

TOOLKIT
- Cold chisel
- Ball-peen or hand-drilling hammer
- Stiff brush
- Paintbrush for bonding agent
- Pointing trowel
- Hawk
- Whisk broom (optional)

1 Chiseling out the crack

Some concrete-patching compounds do not need any surface preparation; others require that you chisel out the crack. Use a narrow-blade cold chisel and a ball-peen or hand-drilling hammer to chip away any damaged concrete *(right)*; wear work gloves and eye protection. Chisel out the crack to about $1/4$" in width and $1/2$" deep; try to undercut the edges as shown at right. If the crack exposes rebar (steel reinforcement), chip out the concrete to 1" behind it. Finally, brush out any loose material with a stiff brush.

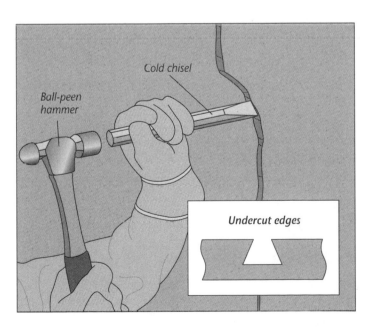
Cold chisel
Ball-peen hammer
Undercut edges

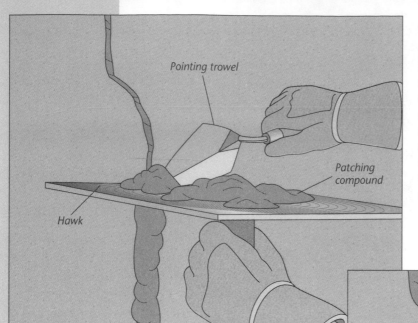

Pointing trowel

Patching compound

Hawk

2 Filling the crack

You'll need a latex concrete-patching compound. Some types may also require a bonding agent—check the manufacturer's directions. Other products may require soaking the crack with water before applying the patching compound. The compound should be thick but not runny. Hold it next to the wall on a hawk and fill the crack using a pointing trowel *(left)*. Work from bottom to top of the crack and pack in a little more compound than the crack will hold. Make sure to fill any space chiseled out behind rebar.

Pointing trowel

Hawk

3 Finishing the patch

Scrape off any excess patching compound with the trowel. Start at the top and hold a hawk below the trowel to catch the material *(right)*. Then smooth the patch with the back of the trowel, starting at the top of the repair. You can use a whisk broom to texture the patch to match the existing wall. Unless you're using a bonding agent, moisten the patch with a mist of water when the edges begin to dry; then cover it with plastic and cure it according to the manufacturer's instructions.

Patching cracks and small holes in stucco

TOOLKIT
• Caulking gun (optional)
• Ball-peen hammer
• Cold chisel
• Pointing trowel or putty knife
• Stapler (optional)

Filling cracks

You can fill hairline cracks with a flexible, all-purpose filler. Or, if the patch won't need to be sanded, you can use caulking compound. For deep cracks, build up the patch with more than one layer, allowing each layer to dry thoroughly. For larger cracks, use a cold chisel and ball-peen hammer to undercut the edges *(page 19, step 1)*; wear eye protection. Brush out the crack, and dampen it. With a pointing trowel or putty knife, fill the crack with stucco-patching compound, packing it in tightly; texture it to match the surrounding stucco. Cure the patch by keeping it damp for about 4 days.

Filling small holes

To repair a small hole (up to about 6" in diameter), first remove loose stucco with a cold chisel and ball-peen hammer, undercutting the edges *(page 19, step 1)*, and blow out any dust—wear eye protection. Be careful not to damage the underlying building paper. If the wire mesh is damaged, staple in a new piece. Dampen the patching site and pack the hole with stucco-patching compound, using a pointing trowel or putty knife. To cure the new stucco, keep it damp for about 4 days.

Patching a large hole in stucco

TOOLKIT
- Ball-peen hammer
- Cold chisel
- Stapler
- Pointing trowel or putty knife
- Finishing trowel (optional)

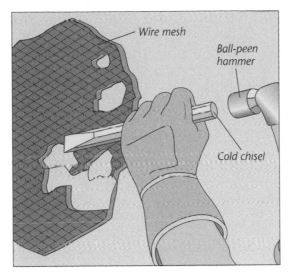

Wire mesh

Ball-peen hammer

Cold chisel

1 Removing loose stucco
Remove loose stucco from the hole with a ball-peen hammer and narrow-blade cold chisel, then blow out the dust—wear eye protection. Staple new wire mesh over any damaged mesh. Spray the damaged area with water.

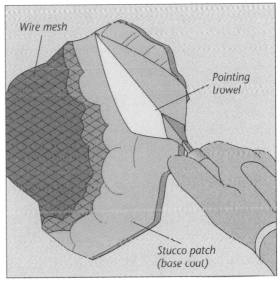

Wire mesh

Pointing trowel

Stucco patch (base coat)

2 Applying the base coat
For the base coat, use 1 part portland cement, 3 parts coarse sand, and $1/10$ part hydrated lime, with enough water to make a fairly stiff paste. Apply the stucco to within $1/4$" of the surface, using a pointing trowel or putty knife; the stucco should ooze behind mesh. When the patch is firm, scratch it with a nail. Cure by keeping the patch damp for 2 days.

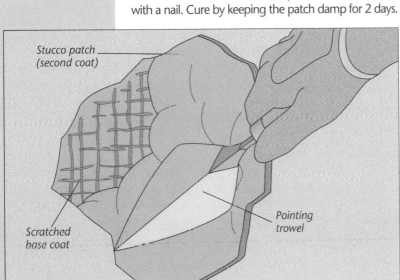

Stucco patch (second coat)

Scratched base coat

Pointing trowel

3 Applying the second coat
Use the same mixture as for the base coat. First dampen the surface of the base coat with a brush or a fine spray of water. Then apply the second coat to within $1/8$" of the surface, using a pointing trowel or putty knife. Smooth the stucco and let it cure for 2 days.

4 Applying the top coat
For the top coat, use a mixture of 1 part portland cement, 3 parts coarse sand, and $1/4$ part hydrated lime. You can add pigment to the mixture to match existing stucco—in this case use white portland cement and sand. Dampen the surface and apply the top coat with a finishing trowel or pointing trowel. Smooth it flush with the existing surface. You can texture it by dabbing a sponge or brush on the surface, or by splattering it with more stucco and smoothing down the high spots. Cure the stucco by keeping it damp for about 4 days. If you plan to paint the patch, wait a month after curing.

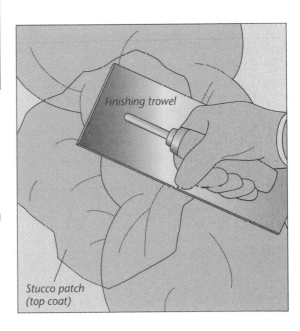

Finishing trowel

Stucco patch (top coat)

In this section, we'll show you repairs for various types of roofs. You'll also learn how to locate roof leaks *(below)*, fix leaky drainage gutters *(opposite)* and patch up flashing *(page 24)*.

Before venturing up a ladder to repair roofing or gutters, it's important to know and observe the following safety precautions. You may also want to look into safety equipment such as ladder brackets and safety harnesses.

If your roof is steeply pitched (it slopes more than 25° or rises more than 6 inches vertically for every 12 horizontal inches—a 6 in 12 slope), call in a professional to make any repairs.

Always try to work on the roof only in dry, calm, warm weather. Check to make sure that your ladder is in good shape, and set it up on firm, level ground, with the base at a distance from the wall equal to 1/4 the ladder's length. While on the ladder, center your body between its rails; reposition the ladder rather than reaching out, and never stand on the top two rungs. To get onto the roof, at least two rungs of the ladder should extend above the eaves. Pull materials up a ladder with a rope and have a place to store them at the top.

Don't walk on a roof any more than is absolutely necessary; you may cause more damage. Don't walk on tile and slate roofs at all—they're slippery and breakable. While on the roof, wear clean, dry, rubber-soled shoes and stay well away from power lines; make sure none of your equipment comes into contact with them, either.

Locating a roof leak

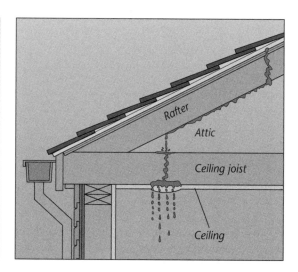

Finding a roof leak

Leaks begin at a roof's most vulnerable spots—flashings, damaged or missing shingles, in valleys, or eaves. Water shows up far from its point of origin after working its way through roofing materials and down rafters to the interior *(left)*. During a storm, trace the course of water to its point of entry. Drive a nail or poke wire through the hole to help locate it later when you get up on the roof (although the nail or wire may be below the actual source), and place buckets to contain dripping water. Once the roof is dry enough, check thoroughly for weak spots.

 QUICK FIX

TEMPORARY REPAIRS FOR A LEAKY ROOF

Roof leaks usually appear during storms, when you can't make permanent repairs. But you can take some steps to temporarily halt the flow of water. An emergency patch (right) can be made by using a putty knife or caulking gun to apply special roof patch liberally to the hole from inside. Work the compound in thoroughly so it adheres.

A temporary shingle (far right) is another solution; replace the shingle (page 26) as soon as possible. When the roof is dry, slide a 2-foot square of galvanized sheet metal under the row of shingles above the missing or damaged shingle.

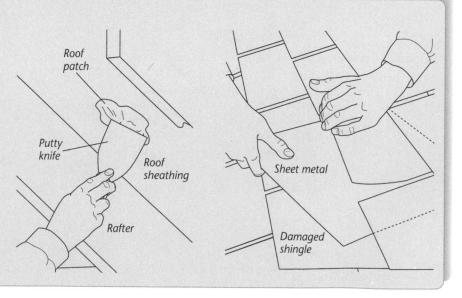

GUTTERS AND DOWNSPOUTS

If you find dry-rotted fascia boards, carve out bad spots and fill them with wood putty or replace the damaged section (apply a wood preservative to the board first).

Tighten any loose gutter hangers and replace broken ones. Check that downspout straps are secured to the walls and that all elbow connections are tight. To avoid water pooling at the foundation, the ground under the downspout outlet must slope away from the house.

Keep gutter troughs clean by removing leaves, twigs, and other debris (protect your hands with work gloves) and loosen dirt with a stiff brush; then hose down the gutter trough. Clean a blocked downspout by spraying with a garden hose turned on full force. Or feed a drain-and-trap auger into it and then flush all loosened debris out with a hose. Add mesh screens over your gutters to deflect leaves, twigs, and other debris. A leaf strainer will admit water and filter out debris.

Patch any leaky joints or holes in gutters *(below and page 24)*, taking care to clean them thoroughly first. Seal pinholes with a dab of roofing cement. If a section of your gutter system is badly damaged, you'll need to replace it.

Repaint the inside of wood gutters as necessary with asphalt roof paint. Sand down rusted and corroded areas of metal gutters and apply asphalt aluminum paint to the inside, rust-preventative zinc-base primer outside. Then paint the outside of wood or metal gutters to match the house exterior *(page 16)*.

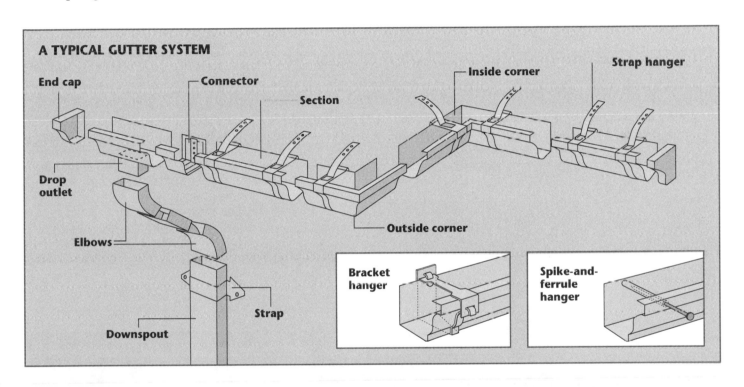

A TYPICAL GUTTER SYSTEM

End cap • Connector • Section • Inside corner • Strap hanger • Drop outlet • Elbows • Outside corner • Downspout • Strap

Bracket hanger

Spike-and-ferrule hanger

Repairing a leaking gutter joint

TOOLKIT
• Caulking gun (optional)
OR
• Putty knife

Sealing the joint
Apply silicone sealant or caulk to the seams where the gutter sections and the connecter meet. Seal both the inside and outside of the gutter.

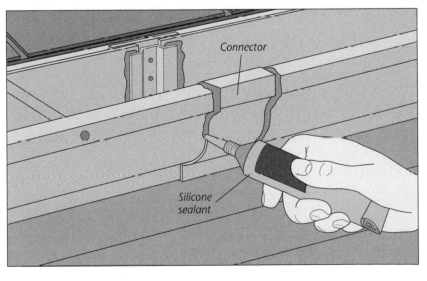

Connector

Silicone sealant

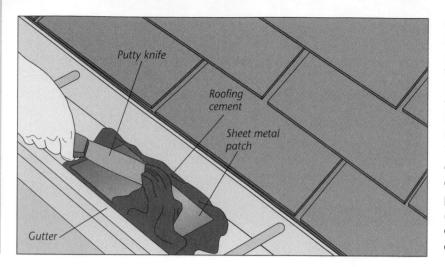

Sealing a hole
For a small hole, use a putty knife and patch with a thin coat of roofing cement, extending the cement beyond the hole in all directions. For a hole larger than 1/2", cover with roofing cement and then embed a sheet metal patch in the cement *(left)*. Apply another coat of cement over the patch, covering the edges.

REPAIRING FLASHINGS

If leaks show up around flashing (sheet metal or roll roofing installed at locations vulnerable to water seepage), it's important to do repairs as soon as possible. (Try to prevent leaks by regularly checking for breaks in the all-important seals at the flashings' edges and resealing them.) Renail any loose nails and cover all exposed nailheads with roofing cement. Also plug pinholes with roofing cement; patch holes up to a diameter of about 3/4

inch with the same material as the damaged flashing: Roughen the area around the hole with a wire brush or sandpaper, then wipe the flashing clean. Cut a patch of flashing material 2 inches larger than the hole on all sides. Apply roofing cement to the area; press the patch in place and hold it for several minutes. Cover the patch with another coat of cement. Have a professional replace any flashing that has larger holes or is badly corroded.

Repairing flashings

TOOLKIT
For valleys or skylights:
• Putty knife
For chimneys:
• Cold chisel and ball-peen hammer
• Caulking gun

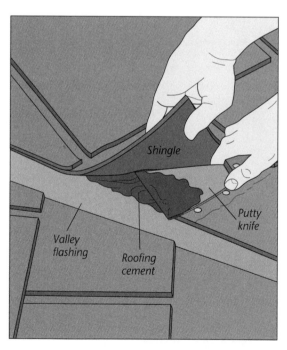

Restoring chimney flashings
Chip out old mortar and caulking along the cap flashing using a cold chisel and a ball-peen hammer. Caulk joints between chimney and cap flashing and between cap and step flashings *(right)*.

Fixing valley flashings
Lift the edges of the shingles along the flashing and use a putty knife to spread roofing cement on the flashing to about 6" in from the edges of the shingles *(left)*.

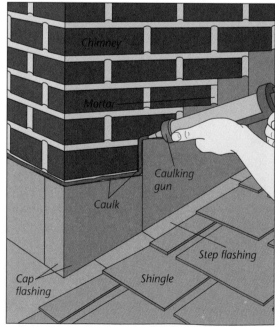

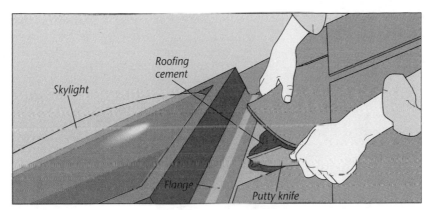

Repairing a self-flashing skylight
Lift adjacent shingles (this may prove difficult) and liberally spread roofing cement between the skylight flange and the roofing felt with a putty knife (left).

ASPHALT SHINGLES

Asphalt shingles last from 15 to 25 years, depending on their composition and the climate. Aging shingles may show bald spots. A heavy accumulation of granules in the gutters indicates crumbling. Check your roof's condition on a warm day when the shingles are flexible (cold shingles are brittle and break easily). Remove a tiny piece of the corner from one or two shingles on each roof plane; the core of the shingle should be black. Gently bend several shingles back to see if they're flexible. If a number of shingles appear gray and bloated, if the material crumbles easily, or if you see large bare spots or damaged areas, consider having the roof redone.

Cracked, torn, or curled shingles can be repaired, as shown below; you should also replace any loose or missing nails. If some of the shingles are badly worn or damaged, you should replace them (page 26). Fasten the new shingles with galvanized roofing nails that are long enough to penetrate all roofing layers (at least 1¹/₂ inches in length). Don't remove a damaged shingle that's located on a ridge or along a hip; instead, nail each corner in place. Then apply roofing cement to the bottom of a new shingle and place it on top of the defective one. Nail each corner, then cover the nailheads with roofing cement.

Repairing an asphalt shingle

TOOLKIT
• Putty knife
• Hammer

Fixing cracks and tears
Seal a very fine crack with roofing cement. Apply the cement along the crack with a putty knife.

For a tear, liberally apply roofing cement under it. Press the shingle in place; secure each side with roofing nails, then cover the nails and the tear with roofing cement (right).

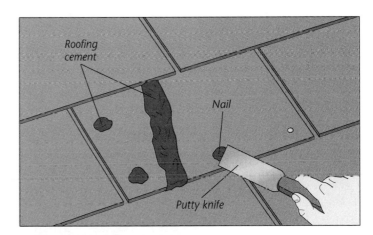

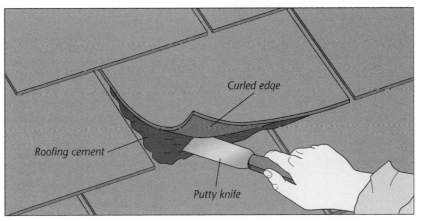

Flattening a curled shingle
To flatten a curled shingle, apply roofing cement under the lifted portion (left), then press the curled edge in place. Tack with roofing nails and cover the nailheads with roofing cement.

Replacing an asphalt shingle

TOOLKIT
- Prybar
- Utility knife or tin snips
- Hammer

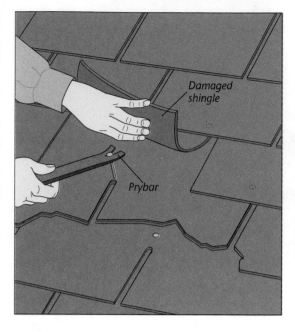

Damaged shingle

Prybar

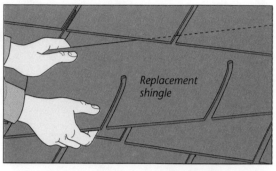

1 ▶ Removing the damaged shingle
Lift the shingle tab above the damaged one and, with a prybar, pry out both rows of nails holding the damaged shingle *(left)*.

Replacement shingle

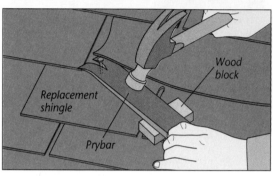

Replacement shingle

Prybar

Wood block

2 ▶ Installing a new shingle
Slide the new shingle into place *(right, above)*, taking care not to damage the roofing felt (snip the top corners if the shingle sticks). Nail on the new shingle; if you can't lift the tab above it high enough to nail underneath, use a prybar to tap it in, as shown *(right, below)*.

WOOD SHINGLES AND SHAKES

Wood shingles and shakes usually last between 15 and 25 years. Inspect the roof for curled, broken, crumbling, split, or lifted ones, as well as for those thinned by weathering and erosion. If only a few are damaged, replace them, as shown below; if the damage is extensive, consider replacing the entire roof.

Replacing a wood shingle or shake

TOOLKIT
- Butt chisel
- Hammer
- Prybar
- Shingle ripper or mini-hacksaw
- Saw

Butt chisel

1 ▶ Removing the damaged shingle or shake
Carefully split the damaged unit along the grain, tapping a butt chisel with a hammer *(left)*. Pull out as much of the wood as possible. Pry up the shingles or shakes directly above the damaged one to reach the nails securing it.

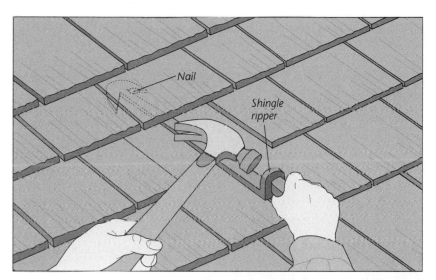

2 Removing the nails

To remove the nails from a damaged shingle or shake you're replacing, either rent a shingle ripper or use a mini-hacksaw. To use the ripper, slide it under the unit and around a nail; then cut the shank of the nail with a hammer blow *(left)*. Be careful not to damage the sheathing or underlayment.

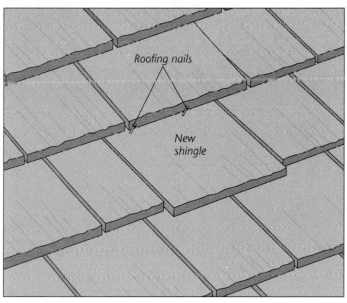

3 Placing the new shingle or shake

Use a saw to trim the new shingle or shake (keep a 1/4" clearance on each side for expansion), then insert it so it protrudes about 1/4" below the adjoining units *(right)*. Drive in two roofing nails at an angle just below the edge of the row above.

4 Driving in the shingle

Drive the edge of the new shingle even with the other shingles, using a hammer and wood block *(left)*. The nails will bend, pulling the heads under the shingles above.

MASONRY TILES AND METAL SHINGLES

Most masonry tile and metal roofs last as long as the house, so problems with them are usually limited to leaks, broken tiles, and dented or damaged metal shingles or panels. Although you may be able to handle small patches or replacements yourself, it's better to hire a professional roofer for any major problems—particularly with ceramic tile, rounded concrete tile, and metal panel systems.

Small holes or cracks in masonry tile can be patched with roofing cement. If the corner or butt of a masonry tile is cracked, clean the area with a wire brush and seal the crack with plastic roofing cement. If the crack extends above the overlap of the tile below, it's best to remove and replace the tile, as shown below.

If you're replacing a tile on a roof where tiles have been laid directly on decking, the job is simple: gently pry up the appropriate tile or tiles in the course above the cracked one, remove the old tile pieces, spread a bit of the roofing cement on the underside of the replacement tile, and slide the new tile into position.

Small holes in metal roofing can be patched like those in metal flashings *(page 24)*; replace a badly damaged shingle *(opposite)*. For extensive repairs, call a specialist in metal roofing.

Replacing a damaged masonry tile

TOOLKIT
- Hammer
- Prybar
- Slip-joint pliers or shingle ripper

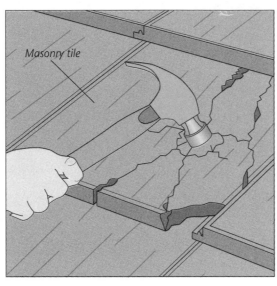

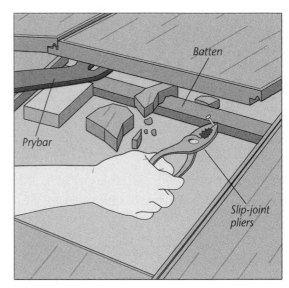

1 **Removing the tile**
Before removing a damaged tile that is nailed to battens, put on safety goggles. Break the tile with a hammer and pull out the pieces *(above, left)*. Be careful not to damage neighboring tiles. Using a prybar, carefully lift the tile directly above to remove shards of the broken one. Remove nails and any remaining shards with pliers, a shingle ripper, or a prybar *(above, right)*.

2 **Sliding in a replacement tile**
Spread a little roofing cement on the underside of the replacement tile and slide it into position *(right)*, hooking it over the batten. Do not nail the tile; its underside hooks over the batten.

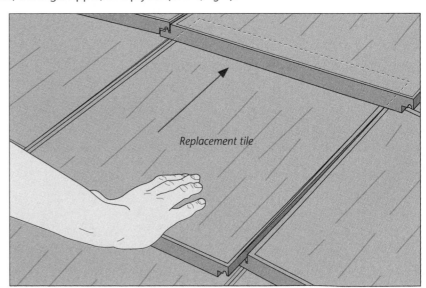

Replacing a metal shingle

TOOLKIT
- Tin snips
- Caulking gun or putty knife

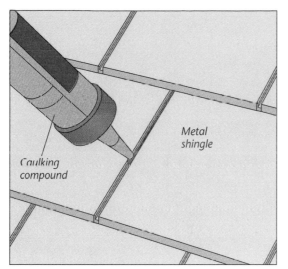

Metal shingle

Caulking compound

Removing and installing a shingle

If you have extra shingles that match the ones on your roof, study the way they interlock to understand how to remove or replace a shingle that's beyond repair. To replace a metal shingle, cut out the damaged one, then trim the interlocking edges of the replacement so it can be slipped into place and hooked to its mates. Be sure to protect underlayment beneath shingles and to seal joints with silicone caulking compound *(left)* or roofing cement (using a putty knife).

BUILT-UP AND ROLL ROOFING

Homes with flat or low-sloping roofs usually have a built-up roof surface. This type of roofing is also known as a tar-and-gravel roof, and usually lasts from 10 to 20 years. Sheds, garages, and other outbuildings are sometimes roofed with asphalt roll roofing, which has a lifetime of about 5 to 15 years.

Leaks in a flat roof are usually easy to locate—they tend to be directly above the wet area on the ceiling. They may develop at flashings *(page 24)* or where gravel has blown away to expose the surface. Leaks are also likely where weather and wear have caused blisters, separations between the roof surface and the drip edge, curling or split roofing felt that's exposed, and cracks or holes in the roof material.

Minor repairs are the same for both built-up and roll roofing, as shown below and opposite; fill in any cracks with roofing cement. If your roof has more serious problems, consult a professional roofer.

Fixing a blister in built-up or roll roofing

TOOLKIT
- Stiff broom
- Utility knife
- Putty knife
- Hammer

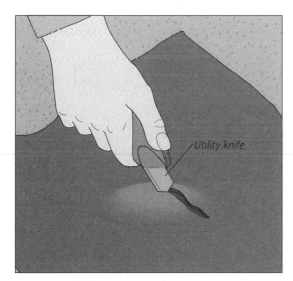

Utility knife

1 ▸ Slitting the blister
Sweep the gravel from the blistered area with a stiff-bristled broom. Then use a utility knife to cut into the asphalt and roofing felt until the pressure under the blister is released *(left)*.

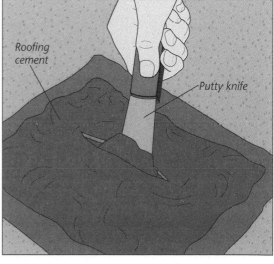

Roofing cement

Putty knife

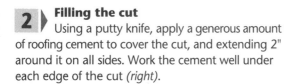

2 ▸ Filling the cut
Using a putty knife, apply a generous amount of roofing cement to cover the cut, and extending 2" around it on all sides. Work the cement well under each edge of the cut *(right)*.

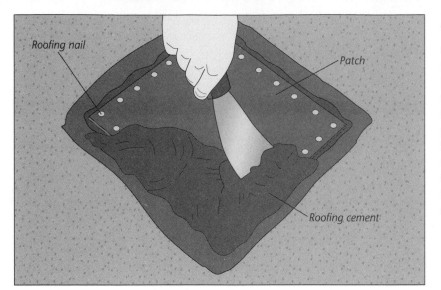

3 ▶ Applying a patch

Cut a patch of roll roofing or asphalt shingle 2" larger on all sides than the slit and press it into the roofing cement. Use galvanized roofing nails to secure the patch, then cover the area with more cement *(left)*. Replace the gravel once the cement starts to dry.

Roofing nail

Patch

Roofing cement

Patching a hole in built-up or roll roofing

TOOLKIT
• Stiff broom
• Utility knife
• Straightedge
• Hammer
• Putty knife

1 ▶ Cutting out the damage

Any hole larger than a square foot should be patched by a professional roofer. Otherwise, sweep all gravel aside, using a stiff-bristled broom; then cut out a rectangle around the damaged layers of roofing *(right)*. Remove the pieces, then cut a patch of roll roofing or asphalt shingle to fit the rectangle exactly.

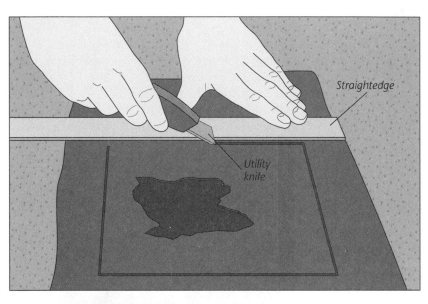

Straightedge

Utility knife

2 ▶ Patching the hole

Fill the hole with roofing cement, spreading it over the surrounding area; place the patch over the cut-out area and use galvanized roofing nails to fix it in place *(left)*. Cover the patch with more cement, extending 2" beyond the edge of the patch. Cut a second patch 2" larger than the first on all sides. Nail it in place and cover with another coat of roofing cement. Replace the gravel once the cement begins to dry.

ROOFING CEMENT

Patch

INDOOR REPAIRS

A house is a complex structure, and with the passage of the years countless things can go wrong. You can't be prepared to deal with them all. However, many minor problems will tend to come up time and time again. This chapter will show you how to deal with many of the problems that are most likely to occur inside your house, from leaky faucets to squeaky floor boards; if you master these common repairs, you'll rarely need to call on a professional.

The plumbing and electrical systems are the veins and nerves of your house. A clogged drain or a blown fuse requires immediate attention. The sections on plumbing *(page 32)* and electricity *(page 48)* will show you how to respond to these situations as well as how to carry out a number of less urgent repairs such as fixing a running toilet or replacing a lamp socket.

Minor damage to the interior skin of your home—walls, ceilings, and floors—can be unsightly. Repairing small holes in wallboard, split floorboards, or bubbles in floor tiles greatly improves the appearance of your home. Sections on walls and ceilings *(page 56)* and floors *(page 65)* are followed by a short section on repairing stairs *(page 71)*.

Doors and windows have a number of working parts—such as hinges, locksets, rollers, and tracks—that can get out of alignment and fail to work properly. In the section on doors *(page 75)* we'll show you how to repair hinged, sliding, and garage doors. Window repairs begin on page 88.

With this chapter as your guide, you should finally be able to take on all those small jobs that are waiting for attention around your home.

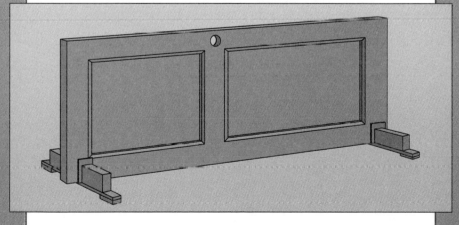

A binding door often needs to be planed. Planing itself is not difficult, but supporting the door can be tricky. Here, a door is supported by 2x4 wood blocks nailed to strips of plywood.

PLUMBING

Your plumbing system has three parts: The supply system carries clean water to your home's fixtures (sinks, tubs, and toilets), and to such appliances as the dishwasher and washing machine. The drain-waste system carries used water and waste out into a sewer or septic tank. The vent system carries away sewer gases and maintains proper pressure inside the drainpipes.

This section begins with instructions on how to clear clogged drains and toilets. Clearing clogs requires that you work with the drain-waste system. Most of the repairs on the following pages—for faucets, toilets, and pipes—involve working with clean water from the supply system. To turn off the water for a repair, refer to the instructions on page 8.

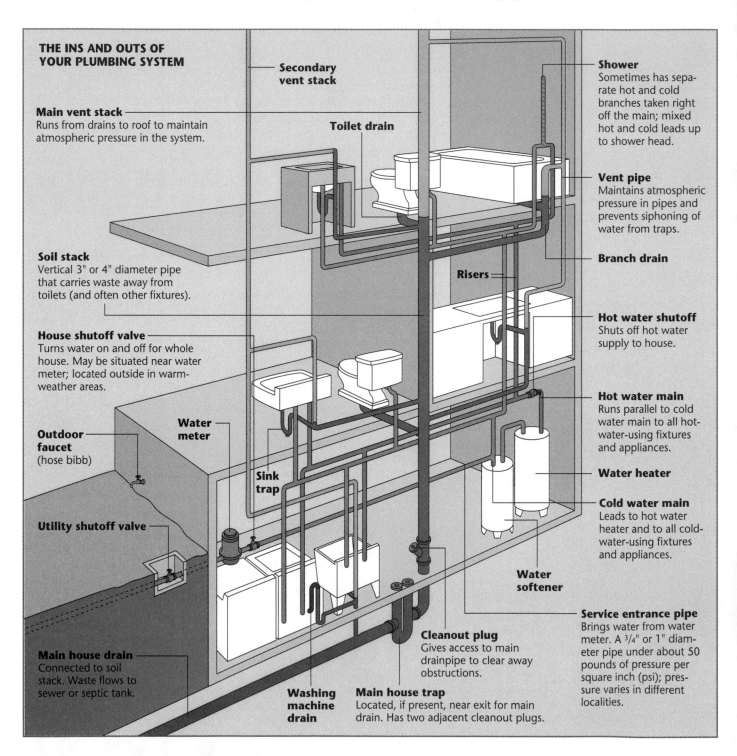

THE INS AND OUTS OF YOUR PLUMBING SYSTEM

Secondary vent stack

Main vent stack
Runs from drains to roof to maintain atmospheric pressure in the system.

Toilet drain

Shower
Sometimes has separate hot and cold branches taken right off the main; mixed hot and cold leads up to shower head.

Vent pipe
Maintains atmospheric pressure in pipes and prevents siphoning of water from traps.

Branch drain

Soil stack
Vertical 3" or 4" diameter pipe that carries waste away from toilets (and often other fixtures).

Risers

Hot water shutoff
Shuts off hot water supply to house.

House shutoff valve
Turns water on and off for whole house. May be situated near water meter; located outside in warm-weather areas.

Hot water main
Runs parallel to cold water main to all hot-water-using fixtures and appliances.

Outdoor faucet
(hose bibb)

Water meter

Water heater

Sink trap

Utility shutoff valve

Cold water main
Leads to hot water heater and to all cold-water-using fixtures and appliances.

Water softener

Service entrance pipe
Brings water from water meter. A 3/4" or 1" diameter pipe under about 50 pounds of pressure per square inch (psi); pressure varies in different localities.

Main house drain
Connected to soil stack. Waste flows to sewer or septic tank.

Washing machine drain

Cleanout plug
Gives access to main drainpipe to clear away obstructions.

Main house trap
Located, if present, near exit for main drain. Has two adjacent cleanout plugs.

CLEARING BLOCKED DRAINS AND TOILETS

Chemical drain cleaners can be used periodically to prevent clogs; they should not be used to clear clogs, as they leave you with toxic fluid to deal with. Instead, rely on two drain-cleaning tools—the plunger and the auger. There are two types of plungers available—one for sinks and one for toilets. There are also two types of augers—one for drains and traps, and a special one for toilets. Turn to page 11 for illustrations of these tools. Because clearing clogs involves working with waste, be sure to wear rubber gloves.

The first step in clearing a clog is locating it. If only one fixture is backed up, the clog is likely near that fixture. If it's a sink that's blocked, first try a sink plunger. If the plunger doesn't clear the clog, try a drain-and-trap auger—first through the drain, then through the cleanout, and finally through the drainpipe. If a toilet is clogged, try a toilet plunger, and then a toilet auger. Tub drains can be cleared with a drain-and-trap auger, and shower drains with a drain-and-trap auger or a garden hose.

If more than one fixture is backed up or if you fail to clear the clog through a fixture, you'll need to work through the main drain. First try putting a drain-and-trap auger or balloon bag *(page 35)* through the main cleanout. If this doesn't work, move downstream to the house trap. Refer to the illustration on page 32 for the location of the main cleanout and house trap. If you're still unable to clear the clog, you'll need to call a professional or consider renting a power auger yourself.

Using a plunger

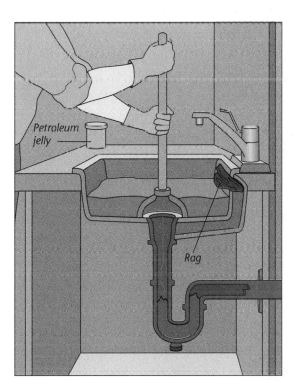

Petroleum jelly

Rag

Plunging effectively

Choose a plunger with a suction cup large enough to cover the drain opening completely. For a clogged toilet, use a toilet plunger. Fill the clogged fixture with enough water to cover several inches of the plunger cup. Then, use a wet cloth to block off all other outlets (the overflow vent, the second drain in a double sink, adjacent fixtures) between the drain and the clog. Coat the rim of the suction cup with petroleum jelly to ensure a tight seal, and insert the plunger into the water at an angle so that little air remains trapped under it. Use 15 to 20 forceful strokes, holding the plunger upright *(left)*; the last one should be a vigorous upstroke, snapping the plunger off and hopefully drawing the clog with it. Repeat the process 2 or 3 times before giving up.

Using an auger

Working with a drain-and-trap or toilet auger

Feed the auger into the drain, trap, or pipe until it stops. If there is a movable hand grip, position it about 6" above the opening and tighten the thumbscrew. Rotate the handle clockwise to break the clog. (NOTE: Never rotate the handle counterclockwise; it can damage the cable.) As the cable works its way into the pipe, loosen the thumbscrew, slide the hand grip back, push more cable into the pipe, tighten, and repeat. If there is no hand grip, push and twist the cable until it hits the clog.

The first time the auger stops, it likely has hit a turn in the piping, not the clog. Guiding the auger takes patience and effort; keep pushing it forward, turning clockwise. Once the auger head hooks the clog, pull the auger back a short distance to free some material from the clog, then push the rest on through. Pull the auger out slowly; have a pail ready to catch any gunk that is brought out. Flush the drain with hot water. Dry and lubricate the auger before you put it away.

Clearing a drain with an auger

TOOLKIT

For a sink drain:
• Adjustable wrench
• Spud wrench
For a shower drain:
• Garden hose (optional)

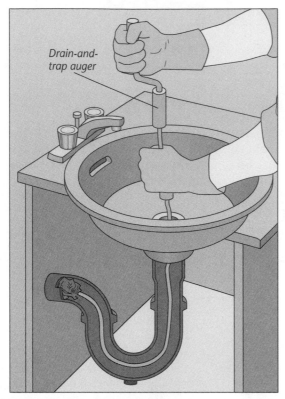

Drain-and-trap auger

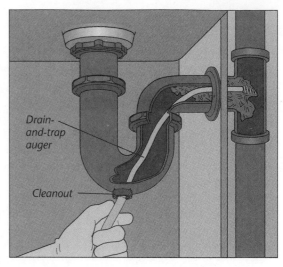

Drain-and-trap auger

Cleanout

Clearing a sink drain

First try putting the auger throught the sink drain. You'll need to remove the sink strainer, unless you can thread the auger through the strainer screen. If your sink has a pop-up, remove it *(page 40)*. Insert the auger in the drain opening, as shown at left; twist it down through the trap until you reach the clog, as described on page 33.

If this doesn't work, try working through the cleanout, if there is one. Place a pail under the cleanout, and remove the cleanout plug from the bottom of the trap. Insert the auger (or a bent wire coathanger); direct it toward the drain, or angle it toward the wall to reach a deeper blockage *(above)*.

Finally, try working through the drainpipe. Remove the trap by undoing the couplings with a spud wrench. Pull the trap downward and spill its contents into a pail. Insert the auger into the drainpipe at the wall as far as it will go, turning clockwise until it hits the clog *(left)*. Clean out the trap before reinstalling it.

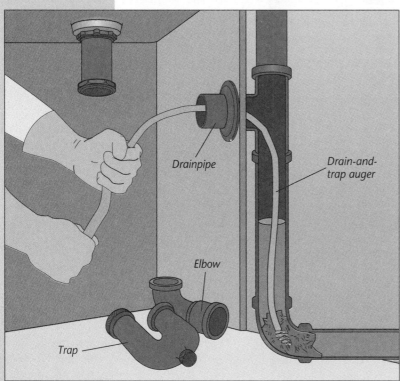

Drainpipe

Drain-and-trap auger

Elbow

Trap

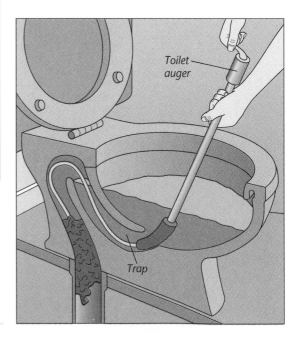

Toilet auger

Trap

Clearing a toilet

To clear a blocked toilet, use a special toilet auger. It has a curved tip that starts the auger with a minimum of mess, and a protective housing to prevent scratching the bowl. Follow the general directions for using an auger given on page 33.

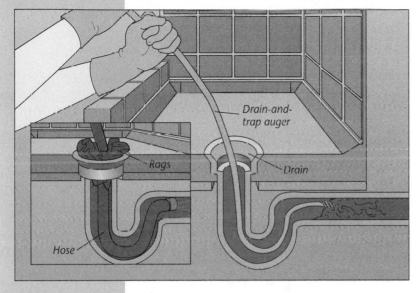

Clearing a shower drain

Unscrew the strainer if an auger can't be threaded through it. Probe the auger down the drain and through the trap *(left)*; operate the auger as explained on page 33. You can use a garden hose instead; use a threaded adapter to attach the hose to a faucet or run it to an outside hose bibb. Push the hose deep into the trap and pack wet rags tightly into the opening *(inset)*. Hold the hose and rags, and turn the water alternately on full and abruptly off. Never leave a hose in a drain; it can siphon raw sewage back into the fresh-water supply. Clean and disinfect the hose when you've finished.

Clearing a tub drain

Remove the overflow plate and pull out the pop-up or plunger assembly *(page 41)*. Feed the auger down through the overflow pipe and into the P-trap, twisting it as described on page 33. This should clear the drain. If not, remove the trap or its cleanout plug from below or through an access panel, and insert the auger toward the main drain. Be sure to have a pail ready to catch the waste.

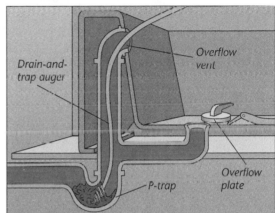

Clearing the main drain

- Pipe wrench
- Drain-and-trap auger
- Balloon bag (optional)
- Wire brush for house trap

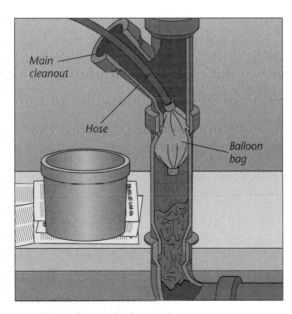

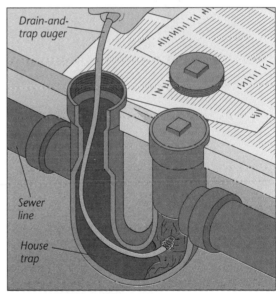

Working through the main cleanout or house trap

First, have a pail and newspapers ready to catch the waste water. Slowly remove the cleanout plug with a pipe wrench. Try using an auger *(page 33)*. If this doesn't work, try a balloon bag and hose *(above, left)*. Never leave the hose in the drain, and be sure to clean and disinfect it afterwards. Flush the cleared pipe with water. Coat the plug with pipe-joint compound before replacing it.

If you can't clear the drain, move to the house trap. With a pipe wrench, slowly loosen the plug nearest the outside sewer line. Probe the trap and its connecting pipes with an auger *(above, right)*. Be ready to take out the auger and cap the trap quickly when water starts to flow. When it subsides, open both ends of the trap and clean it with an old wire brush. Recap and flush the pipes.

Most appliances, valves, and fixtures that use water are engineered to take 50 to 60 pounds per square inch (psi) of pressure. You can determine your water pressure by attaching a water-pressure gauge (below) to an outside hose bibb or to one for a laundry hookup.

Low pressure: The symptom of low pressure is a very thin trickle of water from faucets. Chronic low pressure is typically found in homes on hills near reservoir level. Periodic low pressure may also occur during peak service hours through no fault of the home's location. The only way to increase water pressure to your home is to install a booster system. Flushing the pipes will let through more water by clearing the pipes of rust. Remove and clean aerators on faucets. Close the main house shutoff valve; open fully the faucet at the point farthest from the valve, and open a second faucet nearer the valve. Then, plug the faucet near the valve with a rag. Reopen the gate valve and let water run full force through the farther faucet for as long as sediment appears. Finally, close the faucets, remove the rag, and replace the aerators.

Putting in larger sections of pipe will also give you a greater volume of water. You would need to replace the section of pipe that leads from the outdoor utility shutoff to the house shutoff valve (page 32); if it's a 3/4-inch pipe, replace it with a 1-inch pipe. If you have a water meter, you can also ask your utility company to install a larger one. If you add new fixtures, you may need to install a larger main supply pipe from the point where the water enters the house to the various branches of the supply network, in order to maintain a sufficient volume of water at the fixtures farthest from the main.

High pressure: The symptoms of high pressure are loud clangs when the dishwasher shuts off or wild sprays when faucets are first turned on. High pressure usually occurs in houses on low-lying slopes of steep hills or in subdivisions where high pressure is maintained for fire protection.

If your house has particularly high water pressure, take precautions against appliance damage and floods by turning off the main house shutoff valve (page 8) when you go on vacation, and by turning off appliance shutoff valves, especially those for a washing machine and dishwasher, when not in use.

Above-normal pressure of up to 80 psi can be cured easily and inexpensively by the installation of a pressure-reducing valve. This requires removing a length of pipe on the house side of the house shutoff valve long enough to accommodate the valve and the assembled fittings.

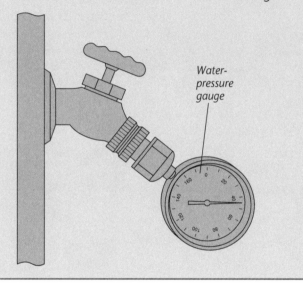

Water-pressure gauge

FAUCETS

There are two basic types of faucets. One is a long-standing design called a compression faucet—usually with two handles and one spout. This type controls the water flow by pressing a washer down onto a valve seat. The other is a more recent type called a washerless faucet—often, but not always with a single lever or knob. In this type of faucet, the flow of water is controlled by aligning interior openings in the handle with water inlets in the faucet body. Washerless faucets come in a number of models. We'll show you how to repair two common ones: a two-handle disc model and a rotating-ball model. In general, washerless faucets are repaired by replacing worn seals or O-rings, or, when necessary, by replacing the entire ball, stem unit assembly, or cartridge. If you have trouble figuring out how to take apart a single-handle faucet, look for a setscrew

under the handle, or a retainer clip hidden under the spout sleeve.

When you're taking apart a faucet, douse stubborn connections with penetrating oil before trying to loosen them. Wrap the jaws of wrenches and pliers with tape to prevent marring visible parts.

Before starting any faucet repair, plug the sink so as not to lose small parts; then line the sink with a towel to prevent scratching the bowl. As you disassemble the faucet, line up the pieces in the order that you remove them so you can put them back together properly. Lubricate threaded parts with silicone grease before replacing them.

CAUTION: Before you work on a faucet, turn off the water at the fixture shutoff valves or the house shutoff valve (page 8), and open the faucet to drain the pipes.

Fixing a compression faucet

TOOLKIT
- Screwdriver
- Adjustable wrench
- Valve-seat wrench or hex wrench for removing valve seat
- Valve-seat dresser

Replacing the packing

If the handle is leaking, disassemble it and tighten the packing nut a quarter turn with an adjustable wrench. Reassemble and turn the water on. If the leak persists, replace the packing (either a rubber O-ring, a packing washer, or graphite-impregnated twine). Lubricate a new O-ring with silicone grease. Graphite-impregnated twine can be replaced with new twine, pipe-thread tape, or IFE packing; wrap it clockwise 5 or 6 times around the faucet stem.

Replacing the seat washer

A spout leak is usually the result of a deteriorated washer or worn valve seat in the faucet. Remove the handle and then use it to turn the stem beyond its fully open position to remove it. If the washer is cracked, grooved, or marred, replace it with a new, identical one. If the washer is beveled, be sure the beveled edge faces the screw head when you install it on the stem.

A TYPICAL COMPRESSION FAUCET

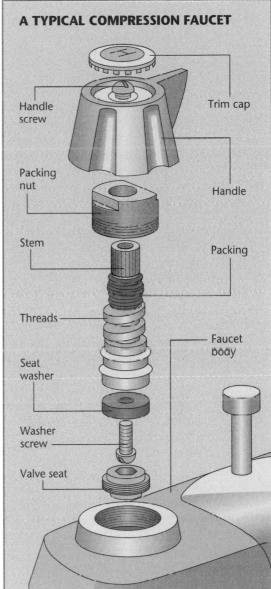

Handle screw · Trim cap · Handle · Packing nut · Stem · Packing · Threads · Faucet body · Seat washer · Washer screw · Valve seat

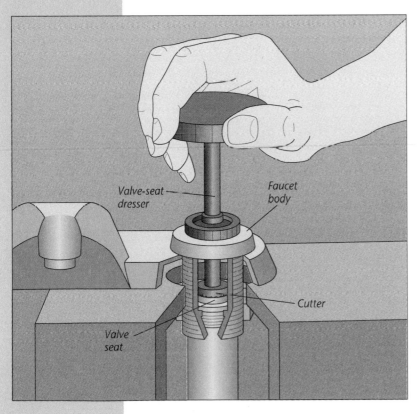

Valve-seat dresser · Faucet body · Cutter · Valve seat

Servicing the seat

If the washer isn't the problem, a damaged valve seat could be causing the leak. You'll need a valve-seat wrench—or the correct size of hex wrench—to remove the old one. Replace it with an exact duplicate. If the faulty valve seat is built into the faucet, use a valve-seat dresser *(left)* to grind down any burrs on the seat. Insert the largest cutter that will fit into the faucet body, and turn the tool clockwise. Remove the metal filings with a damp cloth. After reassembling the handle, let the water run on full for 10 seconds to flush out any filings.

Fixing a two-handle disc faucet

TOOLKIT
- Screwdriver
- Adjustable wrench
- Rib-joint pliers
- Stiff brush or pocketknife
- Long-nose pliers

1 ▶ Disassembling

Pop off the trim cap, if there is one, using a blunt knife or screwdriver. Undo the handle screw and pull off the handle. Use an adjustable wrench to remove the bonnet nut.

2 ▶ Replacing the O-ring or stem unit assembly

If the faucet is leaking from the handle, either the O-ring or the entire stem unit assembly needs replacing. Pull out the stem unit assembly with rib-joint pliers. If the O-ring is worn, replace it with an exact duplicate; lubricate the new ring with silicone grease before rolling it on. If the O-ring is in good condition, replace the stem unit assembly with a new one.

3 ▶ Replacing the seal and spring

If the faucet is dripping from the spout, the seal and spring probably need replacing. Pull out the old parts with long-nose pliers and clean out any buildup in the inlet holes with a stiff brush or pocketknife. Replace the springs and seals with parts designed for the same model of faucet.

4 ▶ Reassembling

To reassemble the faucet, put the stem unit assembly back. Line up the lugs in the assembly with the slots in the base of the faucet. Replace the bonnet nut and handle. If the handle turns toward the back instead of the front of the sink, disassemble it again and rotate the stem unit assembly half a turn.

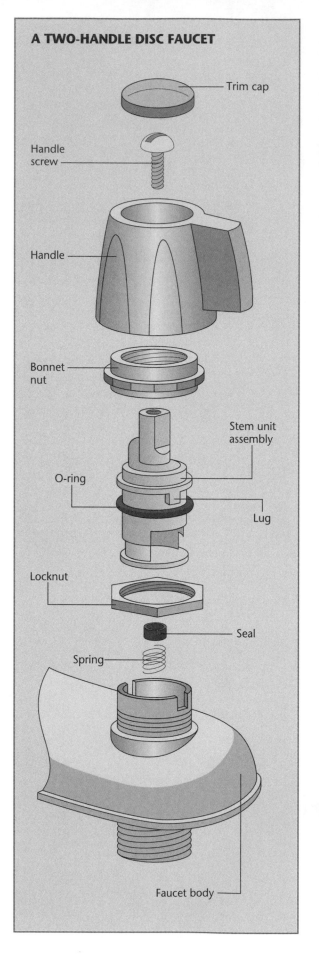

A TWO-HANDLE DISC FAUCET

Trim cap

Handle screw

Handle

Bonnet nut

Stem unit assembly

O-ring

Lug

Locknut

Seal

Spring

Faucet body

Fixing a rotating-ball faucet

TOOLKIT
- Hex wrench
- Rib-joint pliers
- Long-nose pliers
- Stiff brush or pocketknife

A ROTATING-BALL FAUCET

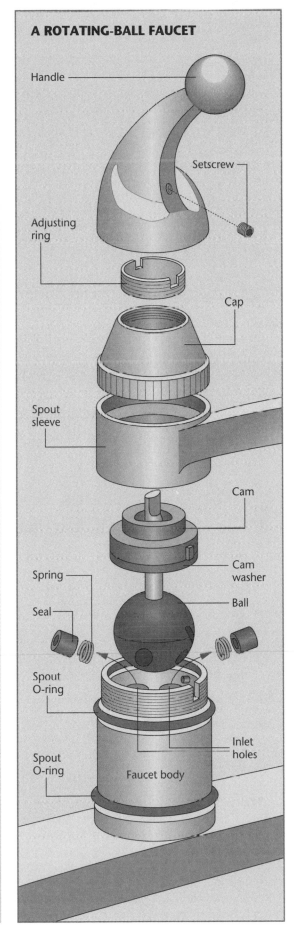

- Handle
- Setscrew
- Adjusting ring
- Cap
- Spout sleeve
- Cam
- Cam washer
- Spring
- Ball
- Seal
- Spout O-ring
- Inlet holes
- Spout O-ring
- Faucet body

1 Disassembling
Loosen the setscrew with a hex wrench and remove the handle. Use taped rib-joint pliers to unscrew the cap. Lift out the ball-and-cam assembly. Underneath are two inlet seals on springs. Remove the spout sleeve to expose the faucet body.

2 Replacing seals, springs, and O-rings
For a dripping spout, replace worn seals. Use long-nose pliers to lift out the old seals and springs. With a stiff brush or pocketknife, remove any buildup in the inlet holes. Install exact replacement springs and seals. For a leak at the base of the spout, replace worn spout O-rings; apply silicone grease thinly to the new O-rings before installing.

⏱ QUICK FIX

STOPPING A LEAKING HANDLE
To stop a leaking handle, remove the handle and tighten the adjusting ring with a special wrench, as shown below, or with a kitchen knife. Put the handle back on. If this doesn't work, disassemble the faucet further and replace the cam washer.

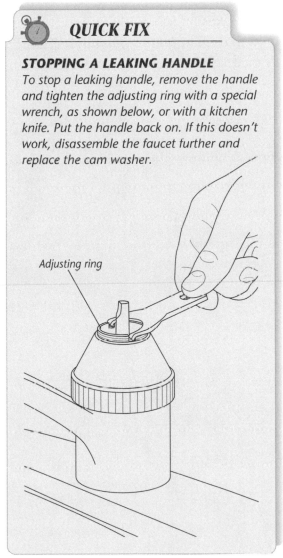

Adjusting ring

POP-UP STOPPERS

Instead of a rubber stopper on a chain, we are now more likely to plug our sinks or tubs with a pop-up assembly that moves up and is set by a lift rod which works through a pivot rod to raise or lower the stopper. The major stopper problem is a bad fit between the stopper and the sink or tub, caused either by a damaged rubber seal or by a misadjustment of the lift rod and clevis. When adjusted properly, the pivot rod should slope slightly downward from the clevis to the drain when the stopper is down.

A tub pop-up works through a striker rod that controls a spring resting on a rocker arm attached to the end of the pop-up. If a pop-up is badly seated, adjust the middle link between the striker rod and the spring.

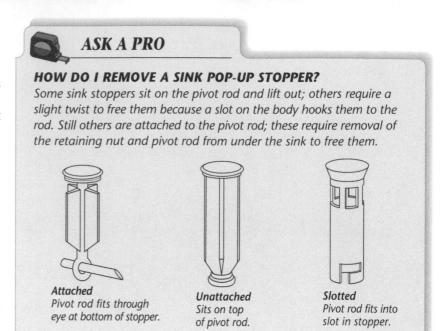

ASK A PRO

HOW DO I REMOVE A SINK POP-UP STOPPER?
Some sink stoppers sit on the pivot rod and lift out; others require a slight twist to free them because a slot on the body hooks them to the rod. Still others are attached to the pivot rod; these require removal of the retaining nut and pivot rod from under the sink to free them.

Attached
Pivot rod fits through eye at bottom of stopper.

Unattached
Sits on top of pivot rod.

Slotted
Pivot rod fits into slot in stopper.

Fixing a sink pop-up

TOOLKIT
- Screwdriver
- Rib-joint pliers

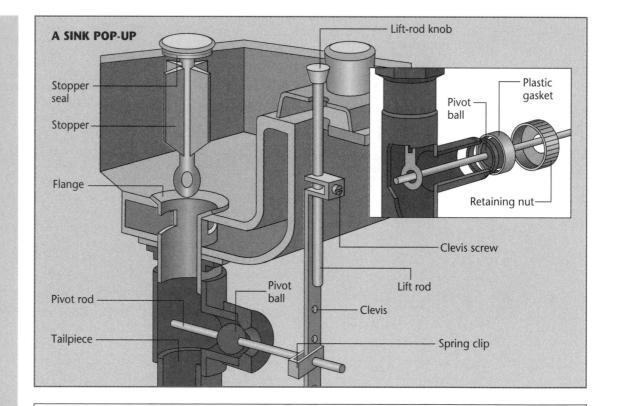

A SINK POP-UP

- Lift-rod knob
- Stopper seal
- Stopper
- Plastic gasket
- Pivot ball
- Flange
- Retaining nut
- Clevis screw
- Lift rod
- Pivot rod
- Pivot ball
- Clevis
- Tailpiece
- Spring clip

Adjusting the assembly
If the pop-up stopper isn't seating snugly, pull it out and remove any hair or debris. If its rubber seal is damaged, pry it off and slip on a new one. If the pop-up still doesn't seat correctly, loosen the clevis screw, push the stopper down, and retighten the screw higher up.

If the stopper doesn't open far enough for proper drainage, loosen the clevis screw and retighten it lower on the lift rod; if there isn't enough room on the rod, move the spring clip and pivot rod to a lower hole.

If water drips from around the pivot ball, try tightening the retaining nut that holds the ball in place; use rib-joint pliers. Still leaking? Replace the retaining nut and adjust the pivot rod so the pop-up seats properly.

Fixing a tub pop-up

TOOLKIT
• Screwdriver
• Adjustable wrench

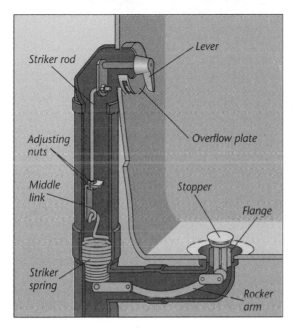

Striker rod
Lever
Adjusting nuts
Overflow plate
Middle link
Stopper
Flange
Striker spring
Rocker arm

Adjusting the assembly
Remove the pop-up stopper and rocker arm by pulling the stopper straight up. Then unscrew and remove the tub's overflow plate and pull the entire assembly out through the overflow. If the stopper doesn't seat properly, loosen the adjusting nuts and slide the middle link up to shorten the striker rod. The striker spring rests unattached on top of the rocker arm. For a sluggish drain, on the other hand, lower the link to lengthen the assembly. Before reassembling, clean the pop-up stopper. NOTE: Instead of a pop-up assembly, some tubs have a strainer and internal plunger that blocks the back of the drain to stop the flow of water. The adjustments to the lift mechanism are identical.

FIXTURES

Simple cosmetic repairs will extend the life of a stained, chipped, or cracked fixture. Liquid chlorine bleach will remove many stains. A mixture of cream of tartar and hydrogen peroxide will improve an enameled fixture. For rust-stained porcelain or fiberglass, try lemon juice or an iron-removing chemical. To cover scratches and chips in porcelain or fiberglass, build up thin coats of enamel or epoxy paint (available in many matching colors). Glue large chips if you have the broken piece.

One of the most common bathroom repairs is sealing cracks in the joint between the bathtub and the wall. The simplest method is to use flexible waterproof caulking compound, commonly called plastic tub and tile caulk, or silicone rubber sealant; you may need to repeat this repair annually as the tub shifts its position. You can also cover the crack with tiles, but you may still need to apply caulk or sealant to the bottom edge of the tiles from time to time.

Sealing the tub

TOOLKIT
• Putty knife
• Caulking gun (optional)

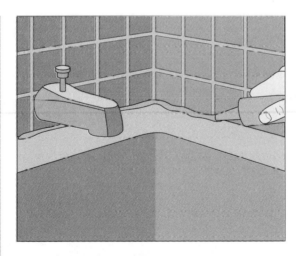

1 ▶ Applying caulk or sealant
Before applying the caulk or sealant, scrape away the old caulk. Clean and dry the area thoroughly to ensure a good seal. Holding the tube at a 45° angle, slowly squeeze the caulk or sealant into the tub joint (left), using a steady, continuous motion. If you can do each side of the tub without stopping, the line of caulk or sealant will be smoother and neater. Wait at least 24 hours before using the tub.

2 ▶ Applying edging tiles
If you find the caulk or sealant won't last in the bathtub-wall joint, you can apply quarter-round ceramic edging tiles, shown at right. Available in kits, the tiles are easy to install around the rim of the tub; use the caulk or sealant as an adhesive. Be sure to scrape away old caulk and clean and dry the area before you begin.

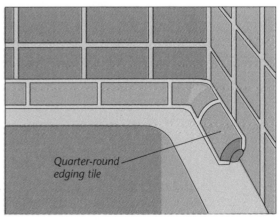

Quarter-round edging tile

TOILETS

A toilet's working parts consist of a flush-valve assembly and an inlet-valve assembly. The first controls the emptying of the tank, while the second controls the refilling; the complete sequence is explained at right. The simplest toilet repair is adjusting the float ball or float cup to set the water level, which should reach within 3/4 inch of the top of the overflow tube. A faulty inlet valve may cause water to run into the tank continuously; solving this problem means replacing washers or seals, or replacing the entire mechanism. A continuously running toilet can also be caused by a faulty flush-valve assembly; the stopper may need to be changed, or the entire mechanism replaced. To diagnose the source of the problem with your toilet, consult the chart on the opposite page. Before beginning the repair, familiarize yourself with the parts involved by studying the illustration below. For information on clearing a clogged toilet, turn to page 34.

Unless you're just adjusting the water level, you'll need to shut off the water and empty the tank. Turn off the water at the fixture shutoff or at the house shutoff valve *(page 8)*. Then, flush the toilet to empty the tank; sponge out any water that is left.

HOW YOUR TOILET WORKS

Here's what happens when someone presses the flush handle on most toilets: The trip lever raises the lift rod wires (or chain) connected to the tank stopper. As the stopper goes up, water rushes through the flush-valve seat and down into the bowl via the flush passages. The water in the bowl then yields to gravity and is siphoned out the built-in toilet trap to the drainpipe.

Once the tank empties, the tank stopper drops into the flush-valve seat. The float ball or cup trips the inlet-valve assembly to let fresh water into the tank via the tank-fill tube. While the tank is filling, the bowl-refill tube routes some water into the top of the overflow tube to replenish the bowl and seal the trap. As the water level in the tank rises, the float ball or cup rises until it shuts off the flow of water, completing the process. If the water flowing into the tank fails to shut off, the overflow tube carries the excess down into the bowl.

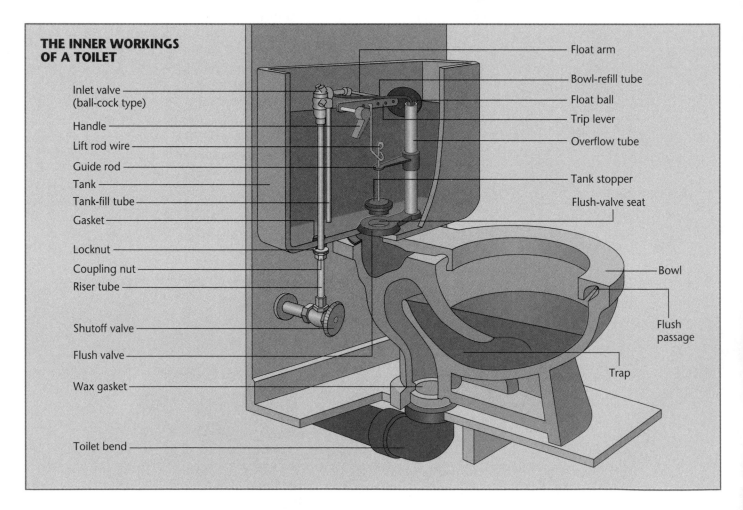

THE INNER WORKINGS OF A TOILET

Inlet valve (ball-cock type)
Handle
Lift rod wire
Guide rod
Tank
Tank-fill tube
Gasket
Locknut
Coupling nut
Riser tube
Shutoff valve
Flush valve
Wax gasket
Toilet bend

Float arm
Bowl-refill tube
Float ball
Trip lever
Overflow tube
Tank stopper
Flush-valve seat
Bowl
Flush passage
Trap

PINPOINTING THE PROBLEM

Problem	It may be...	Try this:
Noisy flush	Defective inlet valve	Oil trip lever, replace faulty washers, or install new inlet-valve assembly (page 44)
Continuously running water	Water level set too high	Bend float arm down or away from tank wall or set float cup (below)
	Water-filled float ball	Replace ball
	Tank stopper isn't seating properly	Adjust stopper guide rod or chain; replace defective tank stopper (page 45)
	Corroded flush-valve seat	Scour or replace valve seat (page 44)
	Cracked overflow tube	Replace overflow tube or install new flush-valve assembly (page 45)
	Inlet valve doesn't shut off	Oil trip lever, replace faulty washers, or install new inlet-valve assembly (page 44)
	Bowl-refill tube continues siphoning water into bowl after the tank is full	Position bowl-refill tube just inside top of overflow tube
Inadequate flush	Faulty linkage between handle and trip lever	Tighten locknut on handle linkage, or replace handle
	Tank stopper closed before tank empties	Adjust stopper guide rod or chain (page 44)
	Water level set too low	Bend float arm up or set float cup (below)
	Clogged flush passages	Poke obstructions from passages with wire
Clogged toilet	Blockage in trap or drain	Remove clog with plunger (page 33) or toilet auger (page 34)
Sweating tank	Condensation	Install tank insulation
Leak between tank and bowl	Loose tank bolts or faulty spud washer	Tighten tank bolts under tank, or replace spud washer
Bowl doesn't refill	Bowl-refill tube is outside overflow tube	Position bowl-refill tube just inside top of overflow tube
Leak at top of riser tube	Loose locknut or coupling nut	Tighten locknut and coupling nut

Adjusting the water level

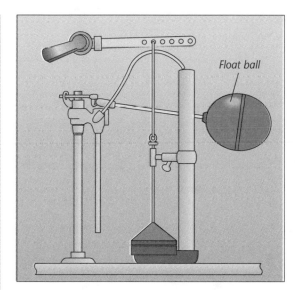

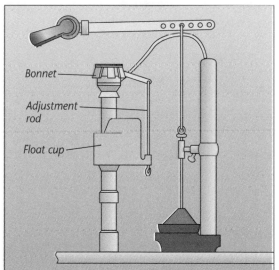

Bending the float arm

If you have a unit with a float arm and ball, bend the float arm up to raise the level in the tank or down to lower the level. Be sure to use both hands and work carefully to avoid straining the assembly. The float ball sometimes develops cracks or holes and fills with water; if this happens, unscrew the ball and replace it.

Setting a float cup

If you have a float-cup valve, move the float by squeezing the clip attaching it to the adjustment rod. Move the cup up to raise the water level, and down to lower it.

Repairing or replacing an inlet valve

TOOLKIT
- Rib-joint pliers

To replace the assembly:
- Adjustable wrench
- Locking pliers

Replacing ball-cock washers

A ball-cock assembly *(right)* is the most common type of inlet valve. Here, worn washers may be the cause of loud tank noises. To replace them, remove the 2 thumbscrews on top of the ball-cock assembly that hold the float arm in place. Lift the float assembly out of the tank. With pliers, pull the plunger up out of the ball cock. Inside the plunger is a seat washer and one or more split washers. If the washers are worn, re-place them with exact duplicates.

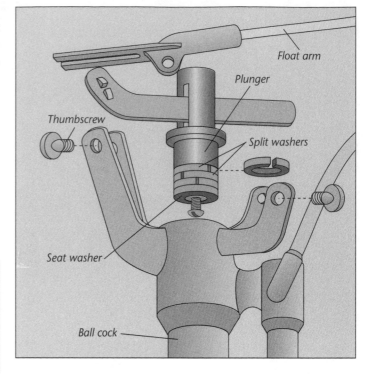

Float arm

Plunger

Thumbscrew

Split washers

Seat washer

Ball cock

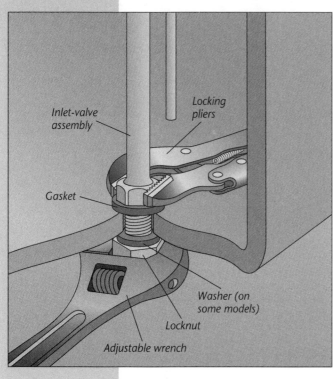

Inlet-valve assembly

Locking pliers

Gasket

Washer (on some models)

Locknut

Adjustable wrench

Replacing the inlet-valve assembly

With an adjustable wrench, unfasten the coupling nut that con-nects the riser tube and the underside of the tank; if the washer is worn, replace it. Remove the float ball and arm inside the tank. Then use a wrench to undo the locknut holding the inlet-valve assembly to the tank *(left)*; hold the base of the shaft inside the tank with locking pliers. Lift out the old inlet-valve assembly.

Buy an assembly that is identified on the package as "anti-siphon" or "meets plumbing codes." First, put on the inside gas-ket and install the new assembly in the tank. Then, put the outside washer and locknut on the bottom of the new assembly. Tighten the locknut (some models may also have a washer). Install and tighten the coupling nut on the riser tube. Place the bowl-refill tube inside the top of the overflow tube; attach the float arm and ball and adjust them as shown on page 43.

Repairing the stopper and valve seat

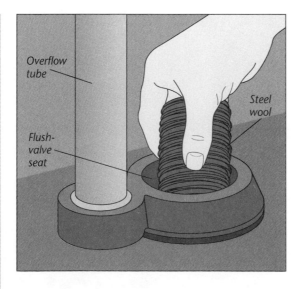

Overflow tube

Flush-valve seat

Steel wool

1 Inspecting and cleaning

A common cause of a continuously running toilet is a defective seal between the stopper and valve seat. To check, remove the lid and flush the toilet. Watch the stopper; it should fall straight down onto the seat. If it doesn't, check that the guide rod is centered over the flush valve.

Inspect the valve seat for corrosion or mineral buildup; gently scour it with fine steel wool *(left)*. If the stopper is soft, encrusted, or out of shape, replace it as described on the opposite page. If the water is still running after the stopper and valve seat have been serviced, you should replace the flush-valve assembly *(opposite)*.

2 Replacing a stopper

If the stopper needs replacing, install the flapper type with a chain to eliminate any future misalignment problems with the lift rod wires or guide rod. First, flush to drain the tank. Unhook the old lift wires from the trip lever, unscrew the guide rod, then lift out the guide rod and the wires. Slip the new flapper down over the collar of the overflow tube and fasten the chain to the trip lever. Adjust the chain with about 1¹/₂" slack with the stopper in place on the flush valve.

QUICK FIX

PREVENTING AN OVERFLOW

If you suspect a toilet is clogged, don't flush it or you'll have a flood on the floor. But if you see an overflow about to happen, you can usually prevent it by quickly removing the tank lid and closing the flush valve by hand; just push the stopper down into the valve seat.

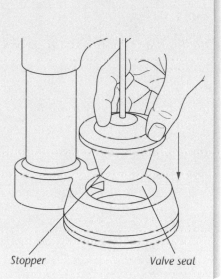

Stopper   Valve seal

Replacing a flush-valve assembly

TOOLKIT
- Spud wrench
- Adjustable wrench
- Screwdriver

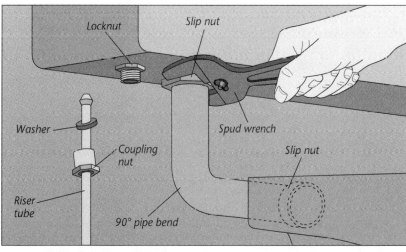

Locknut   Slip nut

Washer

Coupling nut

Riser tube

Spud wrench

Slip nut

90° pipe bend

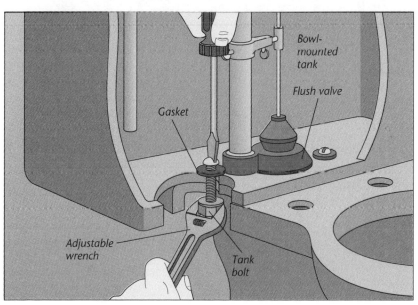

Bowl-mounted tank

Flush valve

Gasket

Adjustable wrench

Tank bolt

1 Disassembling

For an older toilet with a separate bowl and tank, loosen the slip nut on the short 90° pipe bend under the tank using a spud wrench *(left, top)* and remove the pipe. For a bowl-mounted tank, use an adjustable wrench to remove the tank bolts *(left, bottom)*, and then the gaskets. Lift the tank from the bowl.

For both types of tanks, remove the flush valve by unscrewing the spud nut on the discharge tube using a spud wrench; you can then remove the spud washer and flush valve.

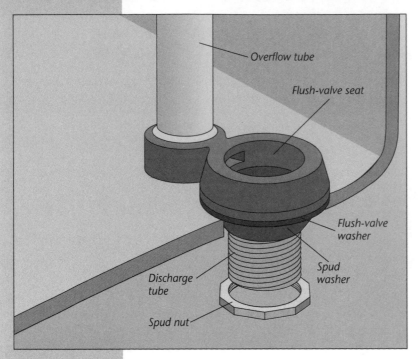

Overflow tube

Flush-valve seat

Flush-valve washer

Spud washer

Discharge tube

Spud nut

2 **Installing a new assembly**
Insert the discharge tube of the new valve assembly down through the tank bottom, with its washer against the tank as shown at left; then put on the spud washer from below and tighten the spud nut to hold it in place. Position the bowl-refill tube just inside the top of the overflow tube.

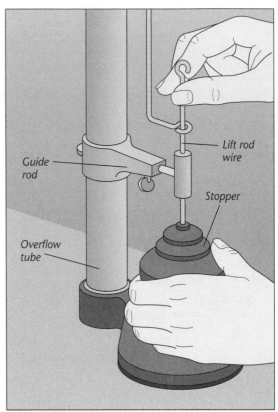

Guide rod

Overflow tube

Lift rod wire

Stopper

3 **Installing the stopper**
If your stopper has a guide rod and lift rod, center the guide rod on the overflow tube over the valve seat and tighten it in place. Install the lift rod wires through the guide rod and trip lever. Screw the stopper onto the lower lift rod wire (*right*), aligning it with the center of the seat. For a flapper type, slip the flapper over the overflow tube, and fasten the chain to the lift rod with 1¹/₂" slack with the stopper sitting on the flush valve. Turn on the water and check for leaks.

PIPES

When water drips or forms puddles near pipes, leaks are obvious, but the sign of a hidden leak may be a high water bill, or the sound of running water when all the faucets are off. First, locate the leak; if you hear running water, follow the sound to its source. Look for stains on the ceiling or walls; a stain on a wall may be lower than the actual leak. If you can't find any stains, check pipes in the basement or crawl space. The ultimate solution to a leaking pipe is to replace it, but pipes can also be patched in a number of ways (*opposite*).

A faucet that won't run is the first sign of frozen pipes; consult the tip at right for ways to prevent or thaw frozen pipes. Pipe noises include load banging, squeaking, and chattering; eliminate these by cushioning the pipe in its support with a piece of rubber, or by anchoring it to the wall with a pipe strap. Water hammer is a resonant, hammering sound when a faucet is closed quickly; the problem can be solved by renewing air chambers or by installing a water-hammer arrester.

ASK A PRO

HOW DO I PREVENT OR THAW FROZEN PIPES?
To stop your pipes from freezing, keep a trickle of water running from the faucets throughout the house. Aim a small lamp or heater at exposed pipes. Wrap uninsulated pipes with newspaper or foam. Install heat tapes (follow the manufacturer's instructions); insulation alone without heat tapes will not prevent freezing, but it helps your heat tapes operate more efficiently. Finally, you may want to keep doors between heated and unheated rooms ajar.

If pipes do freeze, you can thaw them with a heat lamp, heat gun turned on low, heating pad, or hair drier; when using an electrical device to thaw a pipe, make sure it's plugged into a GFCI outlet or extension. You can also try thawing the pipe by wrapping it in rags and pouring hot water over it.

Stopping water hammer

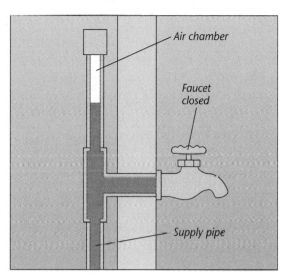

Air chamber

Faucet closed

Supply pipe

Renewing air chambers

Most water systems have short sections of pipe rising above each faucet or appliance, called air chambers. These cushion the shock when a faucet or valve is closed quickly. If air chambers fill completely with water, they lose their effectiveness. To restore them, check the toilet tank to be sure it is full; then close the supply shutoff just below the tank. Close the house shutoff valve *(page 8)*. Open the highest and lowest faucets in the house to drain all water. Then, close the two faucets and reopen the house shutoff valve and the toilet shutoff valve.

If you're tired of restoring waterlogged air chambers, or if your house has none, consider installing patented water-hammer arresters; follow the manufacturer's instructions.

PATCHING PIPES

To patch a pipe, try one of the methods illustrated below. It's a good idea to keep C-clamps and pieces of rubber on hand for emergencies. If you don't have any clamps, you can still stop a pinhole leak temporarily by plugging it with a pencil point. Hose clamps or sleeve clamps provide a longer-term solution, and epoxy putty will stop leaks at joints where clamps won't work.

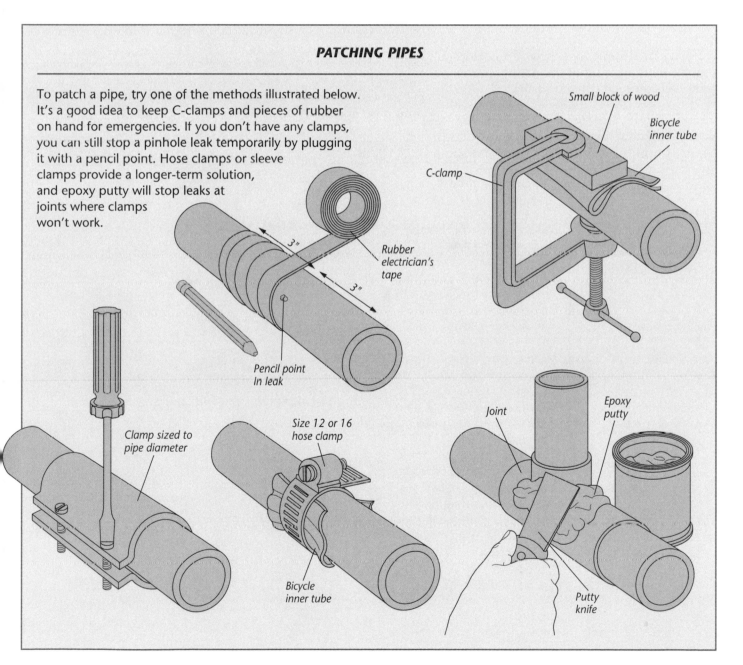

Small block of wood

Bicycle inner tube

C-clamp

Rubber electrician's tape

3"

3"

Pencil point In leak

Clamp sized to pipe diameter

Size 12 or 16 hose clamp

Bicycle inner tube

Joint

Epoxy putty

Putty knife

The *National Electrical Code®* (known as "*NEC®*" or "the Code") contains the rules for wiring methods and materials to be used in electrical work. It forms the basis for all regulations and standards applied to electrical installations. The *NEC* is sometimes amended, so if you move to a new location, check with your municipal building department before beginning any electrical work.

Electricity is a current of tiny particles, known as electrons, which flows through a wire. Important electrical terms include: watts, which are a measurement of the energy supplied by the current; volts, which reflect the potential difference, or pressure, causing the current to flow; and amperes (amps), which gauge the amount of current that flows through the wire or device.

In this section, we'll look at how to restart circuits and replace fuses *(below)*, and how to perform basic repairs to cords and plugs *(page 51)*, lamps *(page 53)*, and doorbells, switches, and receptacles *(page 54)*.

PLAY IT SAFE

PREVENTING SHOCK

Protect yourself from the risk of electrical shock by following these basic safety rules: Before working on circuit wiring, switches, or receptacles make sure that the current to the circuit is off. At the service panel, locate the fuse or circuit breaker that is protecting the circuit; unscrew the fuse or trip the breaker. Always use a neon tester to confirm that you have killed power to the right circuit; if in doubt about what circuit to turn off, shut off the main power supply (page 5).

Current flows in a continuous, closed path from the source, through a device that uses the power, and then back to the source. If you accidentally become a link in an electrically live circuit, by touching a live wire or device, you'll get a shock. It's important to realize that electricity doesn't have to flow in wires to make the return trip to the source. It can return to the source through any conducting body—including a person—that contacts the earth directly or touches a conductor that in turn enters the earth. If you're partially immersed in water, touching any metal plumbing fixture, or standing on the ground or on a damp concrete basement, garage, or patio floor, you're in contact with a grounded object.

Restoring power to a circuit

TOOLKIT

For cartridge fuses:
• Fuse puller (optional)

Resetting a circuit breaker or replacing a fuse

To reset a circuit breaker *(page 7)*, push the toggle firmly to OFF before returning to ON (this may require more force than an ordinary household switch).

To remove a plug fuse, turn to page 7. To replace a plug fuse, either Edison base or Type "S" *(right)*, first make sure that it is the same amperage, then simply screw the fuse into the appropriate receptacle.

Instructions on removing a cartridge fuse *(right, below)* are found on page 6. To replace a cartridge fuse, determine that it is the same amperage and push it against the spring clips until it snaps into place.

A GALLERY OF FUSES AND CIRCUIT BREAKERS

Edison base fuse *(side view)*

(top view)

Good fuse

Blown fuse

Type "S" fuse

Cartridge fuses

Ferrule type

Knife-blade type

Single-pole circuit breaker

National Electrical Code® and *NEC®* are registered trademarks of the National Fire Protection Association, Inc., Quincy, MA 02269.

Testing a circuit

TOOLKIT
• Neon tester (optional)

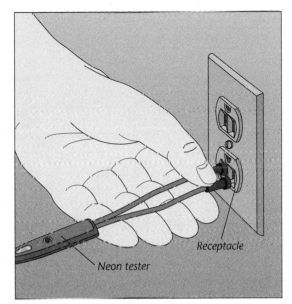

Neon tester

Receptacle

Testing a switch

Grasping the tester leads only by their insulated handles, touch one probe to a hot wire or terminal and the other to a neutral wire or terminal, to the equipment grounding conductor, or to the grounded metal box *(right)*. If the tester lights up, it means the circuit is hot; if it doesn't light up, then you know the circuit is dead.

Testing a receptacle

When you unplug a lamp or appliance because it doesn't work, a neon tester can tell you whether the appliance is at fault or the circuit is dead. Holding only the insulated handles, insert the tester probes into the slots of a receptacle *(left)*; if the tester lights up, the circuit is receiving power. You can also plug in a lamp you know to be working.

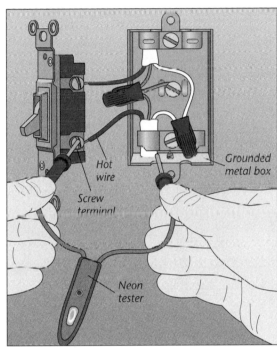

Hot wire

Grounded metal box

Screw terminal

Neon tester

FINDING THE SOURCE OF A SHORT CIRCUIT

If an exposed wire touches a grounded object (a neutral wire, grounding wire, grounded metal box, or grounded metal conduit), a short circuit occurs (current which flows when an accidental path is created between a hot wire and any ground). Cords, plugs, and appliances are the primary sites. Look for black smudge marks on faceplates of receptacles and switches, and frayed or charred cords. Replace the damaged cord or plug *(page 51)* before installing a new fuse or resetting a breaker.

If there are no visible signs, trace your way through the circuit. Turn off all switches and unplug appliances on the dead circuit. Then install a new fuse, or reset the breaker. If the fuse blows right away, pull it out or make sure the circuit breaker is OFF. Remove each faceplate and inspect the switch or receptacle and wiring for charred wire insulation, a wire shorted against the back of the metal box, or a damaged device. Replace the defective switch *(page 54)* or receptacle *(page 55)* or faulty wiring. Then install a new fuse or reset the breaker. (This should be done after every check.)

If the power doesn't go off on that circuit right away, turn on each wall switch, until it does. The short circuit is in the fixture outlet controlled by the switch, or in the ON position of the switch. With power to the circuit turned off, carefully inspect the outlet and switch for charred wire insulation and faulty connections. Replace the faulty fixture or switch.

If turning on wall switches doesn't reveal the cause of the problem, then an appliance is likely to be at fault. Plug in and turn on the appliances one by one. When the power goes off again, you've found the offending appliance. Install a new fuse or reset the breaker. If the circuit went dead as soon as you turned the appliance on, either the appliance or its switch is defective and should be repaired or replaced. If the circuit went dead when the appliance was plugged in, the plug or cord is probably at fault and should be replaced.

If the problem remains unsolved, your wiring is at fault and you should call an electrician to have your electrical system inspected.

A ground fault circuit interrupter (GFCI or GFI) protects against shock. If the amounts of incoming and outgoing current are not equal—indicating current leakage (a "ground fault")—the GFCI opens the circuit instantly, cutting off the power. GFCIs are built to trip in $1/40$ of a second in the event of a ground fault of 0.005 ampere. The GFCI breaker *(right)*, is installed in the service panel; it monitors the amount of current going to and coming from an entire circuit. A GFCI receptacle *(far right)* monitors electrical flow to the receptacle, as well as all devices installed in the circuit from that point forward. The *NEC* requires that receptacles in bathrooms, kitchens, garages, and other damp locations are protected by either a circuit breaker GFCI or a receptacle GFCI.

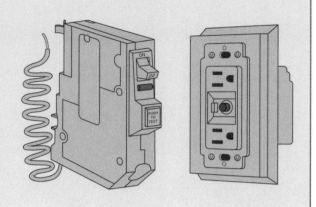

Working with wire

TOOLKIT
- Wire strippers
- Long-nose pliers
- Multipurpose tool

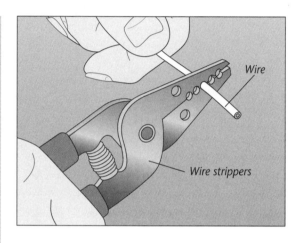

Wire

Wire strippers

Forming a hook
To form a hook, which you will need to make wire-to-screw-terminal connections *(page 52)*, strip about $1/2$" to $3/4$" of insulation off the wire end. Using long-nose pliers, form a two-third to three-quarter loop in the bare wire. Starting near the insulation, bend the wire at a right angle and make progressive bends, moving the pliers toward the wire end until a loop is formed *(right)*.

Stripping wire
Using wire strippers, insert the wire into the matching slot, or set the adjustment screw for the gauge of wire. Holding the wire firmly in your hand with your thumb extended toward the end of the wire, position the strippers on the wire at an angle and press the handles together *(left)*. Rock the strippers back and forth until the insulation is severed and can be pulled off the wire.

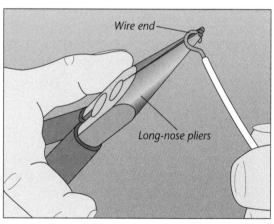

Wire end

Long-nose pliers

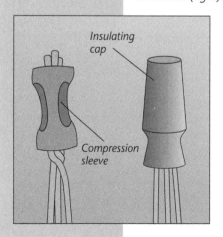

Insulating cap

Compression sleeve

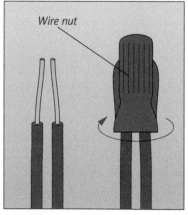

Wire nut

Putting on a wire nut or compression sleeve
Strip off about 1" of insulation from the ends of the wires you're joining. To use a wire nut, you don't have to twist the wires together; simply screwing on the nut twists them together *(left)*. Holding the wires parallel, screw the wire nut on clockwise until it's tight and no bare wire is exposed.

To put on a compression sleeve, twist the wire ends clockwise at least $1 1/2$ turns. Snip $3/8$" to $1/2$" off the ends so that they are even. Slip a compression sleeve onto the wire ends *(far left)*, crimp the sleeve using a multipurpose tool, and put on an insulating cap.

CORDS AND PLUGS

You should always be alert to the danger signs that a cord or plug is in need of repair: arcing electricity, irregularly transmitted electricity, physical damage, or a cord or plug that's too hot to touch. If the cord has frayed or cracked insulation, replace the cord. Detach the cord from the lamp or appliance, and take it with you to an electrical supply store. Buy a length of replacement cord with the same wire gauge as the old one.

The inventory below shows typical flexible cord for lamps, appliances, and power tools. Do not use flexible cord as a permanent extension of fixed wiring.

When replacing a defective cord, also replace the plug. Always replace a plug with bent, loose, or missing prongs, or damaged casing. Self-connecting plugs and those with screw terminals are the most common types. The instructions below describe how to attach both.

Replacing a cord

TOOLKIT
• Screwdriver
• Long-nose pliers

Attaching a new cord
Unplug the appliance or lamp, then access the power cord terminals. Remember that screws can be hidden behind labels, nameplates, or plugs. First, unscrew any screw-on connectors. For cords connected by spade lugs or other connectors, be sure to use the same type on the new cord. If the power cord is attached to the chassis (the appliance body) with a strain relief grommet (reinforcement around an opening), squeeze it with pliers, then push it through its hole. Pull the cord free and remove the grommet, which you will need for the new cord.

Make sure the new cord has the same specifications as the one you are replacing. Reverse the disassembling process to attach the new cord.

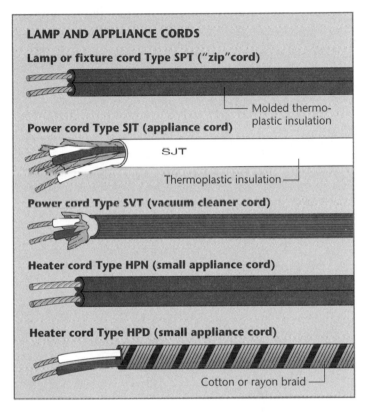

LAMP AND APPLIANCE CORDS

Lamp or fixture cord Type SPT ("zip"cord)

Molded thermoplastic insulation

Power cord Type SJT (appliance cord)

SJT

Thermoplastic insulation

Power cord Type SVT (vacuum cleaner cord)

Heater cord Type HPN (small appliance cord)

Heater cord Type HPD (small appliance cord)

Cotton or rayon braid

Replacing a self-conecting plug

TOOLKIT
• Diagonal-cutting pliers
• Screwdriver (optional)

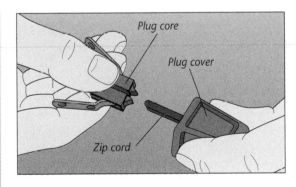

Plug core

Plug cover

Zip cord

2 ▶ **Attaching the plug**
Squeeze the prongs together (right), piercing the cord and securing it to the plug core. Next, slide the plug cover over the plug core. NOTE: Some self-connecting covers do not slide off the core. Lift the lever on top of the plug, insert the zip cord, and press down on the lever to secure the cord.

1 **Inserting the zip cord**
Trim the end of the zip cord with diagonal-cutting pliers, so that the ends are even; do not separate the wires. Separate the plug cover from the plug core; squeeze the prongs or, if necessary, pry with a standard screwdriver between the plug cover and the core. Slide the cover onto the cord. Spread apart the prongs, as shown at left, and push the zip cord into the plug core as far as the cord will go.

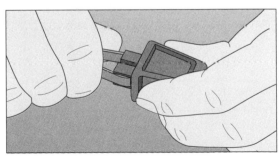

Replacing a screw-terminal plug

TOOLKIT
- Diagonal-cutting pliers (optional)
- Utility knife
- Wire strippers
- Long-nose pliers
- Screwdriver

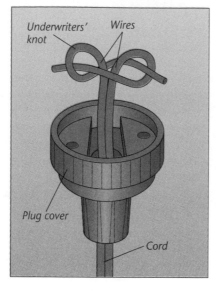

Underwriters' knot / Wires

Plug cover

Cord

1 Preparing the new plug
Use diagonal-cutting pliers or a utility knife to cut off the defective plug. Replace a frayed or cracked cord, as well. Unscrew and remove the new plug's core. With the cord on a flat work surface, use a utility knife to split the end of the cord to separate it into two wires approximately 8" long. Push the cord through the plug cover.

Make a loop with each of the wires, then pass the end of each wire through the other loop. Pull tightly on the wires to form an Underwriters' knot *(left)*. This prevents strain on the terminal screws when the plug is pulled from a receptacle (although you should always pull by the plug, not by the cord).

2 Attaching the cord
Strip 1/2" to 3/4" of insulation from the wire ends (if you nick the wire, snip off the damaged end and begin again). Twist each stranded wire end clockwise, then form loops with each wire end; wrap each loop clockwise three-quarters of the way around a screw terminal on the plug core. Tighten the terminal screws *(right)*; trim excess wire from the wire ends. Fit the plug core onto the plug cover and tighten the screws.

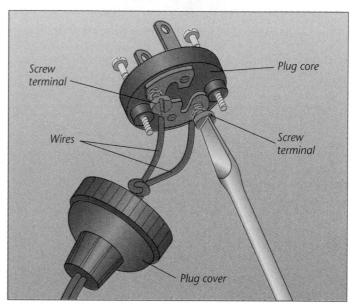

Screw terminal

Plug core

Wires

Screw terminal

Plug cover

Replacing a polarized, three-prong or appliance plug

TOOLKIT
- Wire strippers
- Long-nose pliers
- Screwdriver

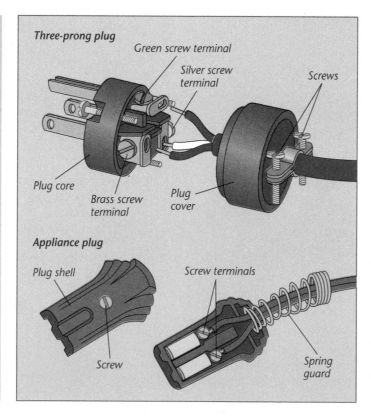

Three-prong plug

Green screw terminal

Silver screw terminal

Screws

Plug core

Brass screw terminal

Plug cover

Appliance plug

Plug shell

Screw terminals

Screw

Spring guard

Attaching the wires correctly
When you're wiring a three-prong plug, follow the procedure for wiring a two-prong plug, attaching the green wire to the green screw terminal on the plug. Appliance plugs look slightly different from lamp plugs, but they are wired in the same way.

For receptacles with one wide slot and one narrow slot, buy a two-prong polarized plug—one with a narrow prong and a wide prong. Begin by stripping the wires 3/4" from the ends. Twist the strands together and carefully wrap each wire clockwise around the loosened binding screw, matching each wire to its corresponding color-coded terminal (follow the manufacturer's instructions). This ensures that the switch impedes the current-carrying wire, and not the neutral wire, reducing the chances of getting a shock.

LAMPS

To repair an incandescent lamp, usually all that is needed is a replacement socket, switch, cord, or plug—however, some lamps may be assembled with rivets and can't be taken apart. On some models of low-voltage lamps, the transformer can be unscrewed and a new one installed.

To replace a bulb which has shattered in its socket, first make sure that the lamp has been disconnected or is on a defused circuit. Press a tightly wadded ball of brown paper bag firmly against the socket, then twist to free the base of the light bulb.

QUICK FIX

ADJUSTING THE SOCKET TAB

If a lamp doesn't work, check that it is plugged in, and that the bulb is not loose or burned out. If you still haven't solved the problem, unplug the lamp, unscrew the bulb, and inspect the socket tab. If the tab is too flat, it won't make contact with the base of the bulb. To raise the socket tab, use a standard screwdriver to gently pry it up, as shown at right. Scrape dirt from the tab with the tip of the screwdriver. If the lamp still doesn't work, replace the socket (below).

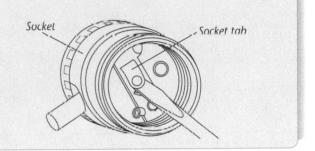

Socket   Socket tab

Replacing a lamp socket

TOOLKIT
- Screwdriver
- Long-nose pliers

Installing a new socket

Unplug the lamp, then squeeze the socket shell near the switch, and lift it off. Pull off the insulating sleeve, loosen the screw terminals and unhook the wires. Buy a proper socket replacement. There is often no need to replace the socket cap; if so, don't undo the Underwriters' knot. Otherwise, thread the cord through the new socket cap and part the lamp cord 2¹⁄₂". Make an Underwriters' knot by forming a loop with each wire. Pass the end of each wire through the opposite loop and pull. Strip ¹⁄₂" to ³⁄₄" of insulation from the wire ends. Loosen the screw terminals on the socket, loop the wires clockwise around the screw terminals, and tighten the screws. Place the insulating sleeve over the socket, then the socket shell. Fit the corrugated edges of the shell inside the cap rim, then push them together until you hear a click. Squeeze the arms of the harp together and slide them into the retainer.

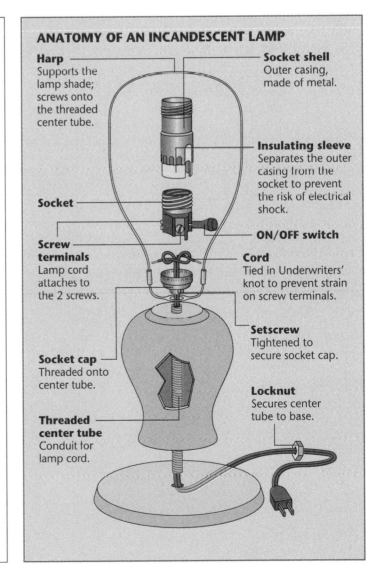

ANATOMY OF AN INCANDESCENT LAMP

Harp
Supports the lamp shade; screws onto the threaded center tube.

Socket shell
Outer casing, made of metal.

Insulating sleeve
Separates the outer casing from the socket to prevent the risk of electrical shock.

Socket

Screw terminals
Lamp cord attaches to the 2 screws.

ON/OFF switch

Cord
Tied in Underwriters' knot to prevent strain on screw terminals.

Setscrew
Tightened to secure socket cap.

Socket cap
Threaded onto center tube.

Locknut
Secures center tube to base.

Threaded center tube
Conduit for lamp cord.

DOORBELLS

All doorbell systems operate with voltage significantly lower than the 120 volts of normal household current. The doorbell circuit is connected to a transformer which brings down the 120-volt current to 6 to 24 volts, depending on the capacity of the transformer and bell.

For most diagnostic work on a doorbell, the power source must be connected. However, to work on the transformer, always de-energize the circuit by pulling the fuse or tripping the breaker. (Remember, the input side of the transformer is high voltage—120 volts.)

Fixing a silent doorbell

TOOLKIT
• Screwdriver

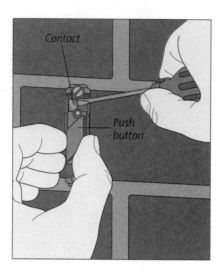

Diagnosing and fixing the problem

Check that the fuse or circuit breaker hasn't blown or tripped. Have someone push the button while you listen to the transformer: If it hums, it's working; otherwise, it may be defective or there may be a break in the circuit. Disconnect the two wires for the push button, and touch their bare ends together. If the bell rings, the button is defective and should be replaced; if it still doesn't work, check for a poor or broken wire connection. Use electrical tape to make any minor repairs to the wires.

Check wire connections at the transformer, bell mechanism, and push button. You may need to remove the button cover or unscrew the button unit from the wall. Using fine sandpaper and a screwdriver, scrape off corrosion from the contacts; clean and tighten loose terminal connections. If the contacts are flat, use a screwdriver to pry them up slightly (left). Reinstall the push button.

SWITCHES AND RECEPTACLES

Replace a switch or receptacle that doesn't work once you've checked others on the same circuit, so you know the problem is not with the circuit. Read the information stamped on your new switch; make sure the new switch (single-pole or three-way) has the same amperage and voltage ratings as the one you're replacing.

Grounded receptacles have an upper and lower outlet with three slots. The Code requires that all receptacles for 15- or 20-amp, 120-volt branch circuits (most of the circuits in your home) be of the grounding type. Like switches, all receptacles are rated for a specific amperage and voltage, found on the front of the receptacle.

When replacing an existing swich or receptacle, take note of its wiring configuration before you detach the wires. You can tag each wire with a piece of masking tape or draw a diagram of the system.

A three-prong plug is grounded to protect against electric shock. If your receptacles are the two-prong variety, you can use an adapter plug. However, this is effective only if the receptacle box is grounded.

Replacing a switch

TOOLKIT
• Screwdriver

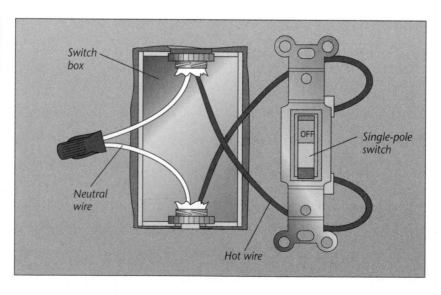

Removing and reinstalling a switch

Turn off power to the switch at the fuse box or circuit breaker. Unscrew the cover plate and the mounting screws. Tag the wires with masking tape or draw a diagram before removing the switch; connect the wires to the new switch in the same way. Screw in the mounting screws and attach the cover plate.

Replacing a receptacle

TOOLKIT
• Screwdriver
• Long-nose pliers

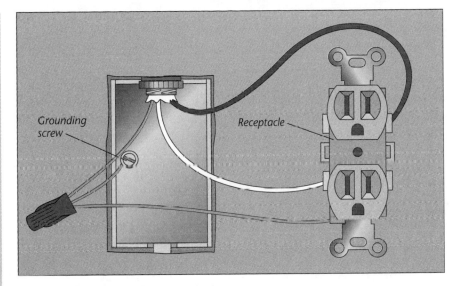

Removing and installing a receptacle

First shut off the power to the circuit. Then unscrew the cover plate and remove it. Next, unscrew the receptacle from its box and carefully pull it out. Note which wire is connected to which screw terminal; then disconnect the wires from the screws.

To install the new receptacle, wrap the wires clockwise around the screws, using the tags or diagram from the old receptacle as a guide. Screw the receptacle to the box, and replace the cover plate.

Installing a grounding-adapter plug

TOOLKIT
• Neon tester
• Screwdriver

1 ▶ **Testing for grounding**
Before installing a grounding-adapter plug, test to confirm that the receptacle box is grounded. With power to the circuit on, insert a probe of a neon tester into a slot in the receptacle as shown, and place the other probe on the mounting screw *(right)*. CAUTION: Hold only the insulated part of the tester. Repeat the testing procedure with the other slot. If the tester lights up in only 1 of the 2 slots of the receptacle, the box is grounded and you can install an adapter plug.

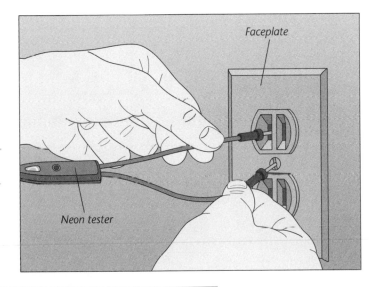

2 **Installing the adapter plug**
First loosen the mounting screw on the faceplate of the receptacle. Plug the adapter into one of the outlets on the receptacle and fit the screw lug attached to the adapter plug under the mounting screw. Secure the connection by tightening the screw *(left)*.

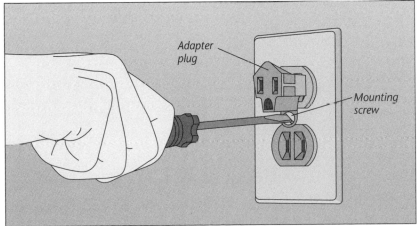

WALLS AND CEILINGS

In this section, we'll tackle wall and ceiling repairs. Fixing gypsum wallboard is easy; follow the instructions below. You'll find out how to repair cracks and holes—big or small—in plaster *(page 59)*, and replace broken ceramic tiles *(page 62)*. Replacing ceiling tiles is not difficult, as you'll see on page 64.

Each type of wall material has its own special needs. That's why it's important to use the appropriate patching material or adhesive. For repairs to ceramic tile in a bathroom, for example, use water-resistant mastic. CAUTION: Before cutting into a wall, determine the location of any wires and pipes that may be behind it.

GYPSUM WALLBOARD

Gypsum wallboard is used as a backing for many types of wall treatment—paint, wallpaper, fabric, tile, and even paneling. Standard wallboard is made of a fire-resistant gypsum core sandwiched between two layers of paper. Some wallboard is water-resistant, for use in bathrooms and other damp areas. Although panels are usually 4x8 feet and 1/2 inch thick, dimensions can vary.

Wallboard panels may be fastened to wall studs or furring strips with wallboard nails, annular-ring nails, dry-wall screws, or adhesive. Usually, joints between panels are covered with wallboard tape and several layers of joint compound.

Minor ills that plague wallboard include dents, small nail or screw holes, and popped nails. You can easily repair wallboard with spackling compound, patching plaster, or joint compound, and a putty knife, a claw hammer, and sandpaper. The repaired area should blend with the surrounding surface.

Repairing a dent in wallboard

TOOLKIT
• Sanding block
• 4" taping knife

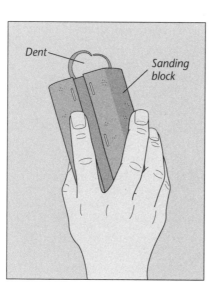

Dent / Sanding block

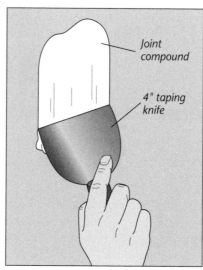

Joint compound / 4" taping knife

Filling in the dent
Sand the dent site with a sanding block *(far left)*. Then, using a 4" taping knife, fill the dent with one or more layers of all-purpose joint compound *(left)*; allow each layer to dry before applying the next. When dry, sand and prime the repair.

Fixing a popped nail in wallboard

TOOLKIT
• Hammer
• Putty knife
• Sanding block

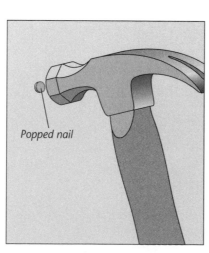

Popped nail

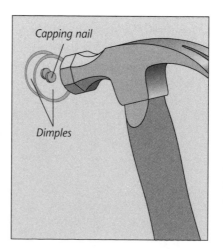

Capping nail / Dimples

Driving in and covering the nail
Hammer in and dimple the popped nail *(far left)*; drive and dimple another nail just below and slightly overlapping to hold it in *(left)*. Use a putty knife to cover the dimples with joint compound. When dry, sand and prime.

Patching small holes in wallboard

TOOLKIT
• Putty knife
• Sanding block

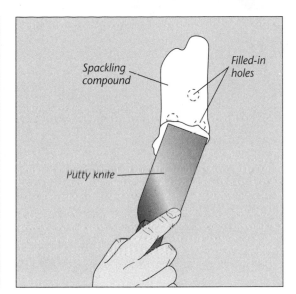

Spackling compound

Filled-in holes

Putty knife

Filling the hole
Brush the holes clean and dampen them with a sponge. Use a flexible, narrow-bladed putty knife to fill the holes with spackling compound or patching plaster *(left)*. When dry, sand and prime.

 ASK A PRO

HOW DO I FIND STUDS?
If you can't locate a wall stud using a commercial stud finder, try probing into the wall in an inconspicuous place about 2 inches above the floor with a nail or drill. When you find a stud, measure 16 or 24 inches from that point to find the center of the next stud.

Repairing a large hole in wallboard

TOOLKIT
• Compass saw
• Utility knife
• Prybar
• Nail claw
• Perforated rasp
• Screwdriver or hammer
• Saw
• Tape measure
• 4" taping knife
• 6" taping knife
• 10" taping knife
• Sanding block
• Paintbrush

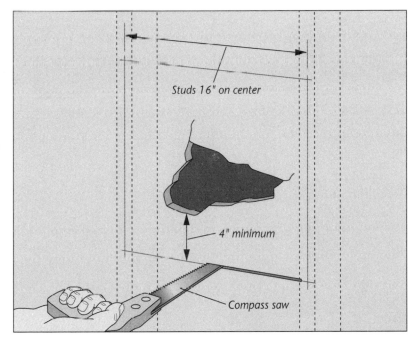

Studs 16" on center

4" minimum

Compass saw

1 **Removing a damaged section**
To remove the damaged wallboard, first locate the wall studs *(above)*. Use a compass saw to cut the damaged section, centering the side cuts over the studs *(left)*; cut the sides and corners with a utility knife. Remove the piece with a prybar; pull out remaining nails.

2 **Attaching a new piece**
Cut a replacement piece as thick as the original; measure and cut it to match the damaged section. Smooth rough edges with a perforated rasp. Screw or nail the new piece to the studs. Load about half the blade of a 4" taping knife with joint compound. Apply the compound across the joint and then draw the knife along the joint at a 45° angle *(right)*. Use increasingly wider knives for each layer to make the joint smoother. (To finish water-resistant wallboard, use water-resistant compound—follow the package directions.) Repeat on all sides.

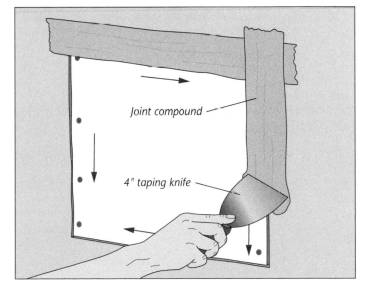

Joint compound

4" taping knife

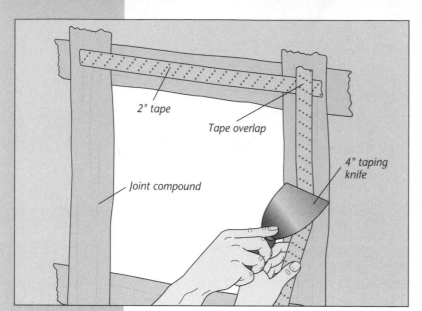

2" tape

Tape overlap

Joint compound

4" taping knife

3 Taping the joints

This step blends the repair with the surrounding surface and is staggered over several days. Center tape over each joint; press down with a 4" taping knife *(left)*. Remove excess joint compound with the knife, feathering the edges. Thinly apply compound over the tape. Let each layer dry for at least 24 hours. When dry, wet the patch with a sponge and sand the compound using No. 600 grit silicon carbide sandpaper on a sanding block. Never sand wallboard—the scratches may show through the finish. Apply a second coat of compound using a 6" taping knife; feather the edges. When the compound is dry, wet-sand the edges to remove minor imperfections. CAUTION: When sanding, wear safety goggles and a dust mask.

4 Applying the third coat of compound

Apply a third coat of compound, using a 10" taping knife held at a 45° angle to the wall *(right)*. Use only as much compound as necessary to cover the previous layer.

10" taping knife

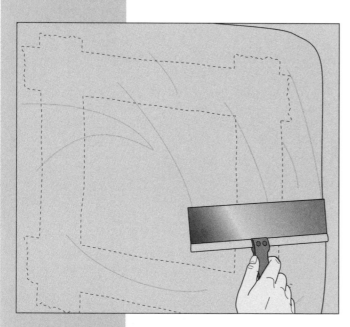

5 Feathering the edges

Using a 10" taping knife *(left)*, feather the edges of the third coat 12" to 18" out. Try to remove any ridges in the compound. Allow the compound to dry before doing the final sanding.

6 Wet-sanding and finishing

Give the compound a final wet sanding to remove imperfections *(right)*. Wipe off sanding residue with a damp sponge and allow the compound to dry. Then apply a primer or base coat of paint, or, for wallpaper, seal it with shellac or varnish.

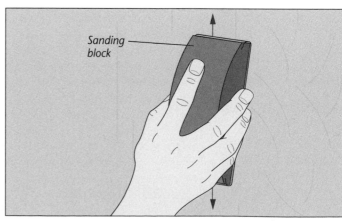

Sanding block

PLASTER WALLS

There are three layers in a plastered wall: a base coat, a thick coat of plaster for strength, and a finishing coat for appearance. These may be applied over wood lath, metal mesh, special gypsum wallboard, or masonry.

On these pages, you'll find instructions for patching cracks and holes in plaster with or without a lath base,

as well as tips on finishing a patched area to match the surrounding surface. To fill a hole without a base (for example, where an electrical box has been removed or where the base is damaged), you'll have to install metal mesh *(page 62)*. If a large area is damaged or the base needs repair, you may want to call in a professional.

ASK A PRO

HOW CAN I MATCH EXISTING WALL TEXTURE?

Matching an existing texture requires skillful treatment of the still-wet finishing plaster. You'll have to experiment to achieve a good match. For a smooth surface, pull a finishing trowel or wide putty knife dipped in water across the plaster. When dry, sand it to remove minor imperfections; prime before painting.

For a textured surface, use a paint brush, stippling brush, household sponge, sponge float, whisk broom, or wire brush. Daub or swirl a uniform, random, or overlapping pattern. To create peaks, use a brush or a tool with bristles; when the peaks stiffen, gently draw a clean finishing trowel over the surface. Let dry; then prime and paint.

Filling a small crack in plaster

TOOLKIT
• Cold chisel
• Putty knife (optional)
• Sanding block
• Paintbrush

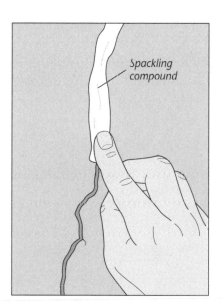

Spackling compound

Sanding block

Applying spackling compound

To repair fine cracks, use spackling compound or a special crack patcher. Widen the crack to about 1/8" with a cold chisel; blow out dust. Use your finger or a putty knife to fill the crack with compound *(far left)*; let dry. With a sanding block and fine-grade sandpaper, sand in a circular motion *(left)*. Prime with sealer before painting.

PAINTING OVER WALL REPAIRS

The type of surface you're covering determines the kind of paint required. If possible, use any paint left over from the original job. Otherwise, ask your local paint dealer about the correct paint for your walls. Choosing the right brush is important, too. The type of bristle should suit the paint or stain you're using; the brush size must fit the job. Select a natural-bristle brush to apply oil/alkyd-base paint, polyurethane, varnish, or shellac. Use brushes with synthetic bristles to apply water-base (latex) paint. For wood stains, use either type of brush.

Choose a 1-inch brush for hard-to-reach areas, a 2- to 3-inch brush for medium-size surfaces, and a 3 1/2- to 4-inch brush or a 9-inch roller for large areas, such as entire walls. Use a thick-napped roller for textured walls.

Before you apply any paint, you may need to sand and wash the surface. In most cases, you will at least have to apply a primer so your repair won't show through. For new gypsum wallboard, you should use a latex sealer; for plaster surfaces, an oil/alkyd sealer with an oil/alkyd paint is recommended.

Patching a wide crack in plaster

TOOLKIT
• Cold chisel (optional)
• Putty knife
• 6" taping knife
• Steel straightedge

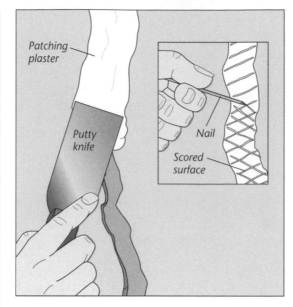

Patching plaster

Putty knife

Nail

Scored surface

1 Filling the crack

Undercut the crack with the tip of a cold chisel or a putty knife to help bond the new plaster; blow out dust and debris. Dampen the crack with a wet paintbrush or sponge. Using a putty knife, apply the first layer of patching plaster *(left)*, which should fill little more than half the depth, leaving enough space for the next two layers. Let each layer dry completely before adding the next. Score the plaster with a nail when firm but not hard to provide "bite" for the next layer *(inset)*.

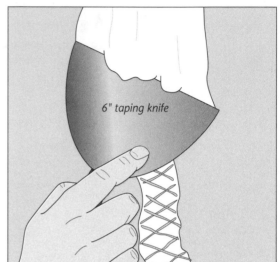

6" taping knife

2 Completing the patch

Wet the dry patch again; use a 6" taping knife to apply the next layer to within ⅛" to ¼" of the surface *(right)*. Let the patch dry before applying the finish coat. Fill with finishing plaster and strike off with a straightedge to remove excess *(step 5, opposite)*; then, finish the patch *(page 59)*. When dry, prime and paint.

Patching a hole in plaster with a base

TOOLKIT
• Cold chisel and ball-peen hammer
• 6" taping knife
• Straightedge
• Finishing trowel
• Sanding block

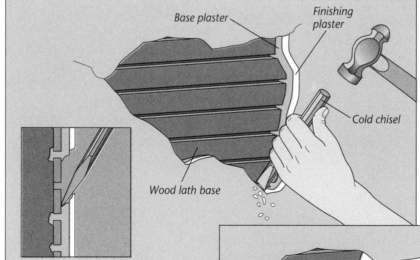

Base plaster

Finishing plaster

Cold chisel

Wood lath base

1 Preparing the area

Remove cracked plaster from the edges with a cold chisel and ball-peen hammer *(left)*. Undercut the edges *(inset)* to ensure a good bond; blow away debris. Dampen the edges with a sponge.

Patching plaster (first coat)

2 Applying the first patching coat

Using a 6" taping knife, fill a little more than half the hole's depth with patching plaster; force it through gaps in the lath *(right)*. Score the plaster with a nail, as shown above, to provide "bite" when firm. Let the plaster dry.

3 ▶ Applying the second coat

Wet the patch again; use a 6" taping knife to apply a second layer of plaster to within ¹/₈" to ¹/₄" of the surface *(right)*. Score the plaster with a nail; let the plaster dry.

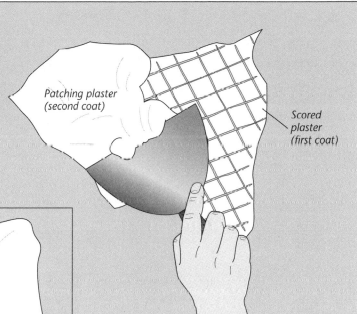

Patching plaster (second coat)

Scored plaster (first coat)

Feathered edge

Finishing plaster

4 ▶ Applying the finishing plaster

Use a 6" taping knife to apply finishing plaster; feather the edges an inch or more beyond the edges of the patch *(left)*.

5 ▶ Striking off the finished plaster

Strike off the wet finishing plaster with a straightedge to remove excess plaster *(right)*. Turn to page 59 for details on making a textured surface.

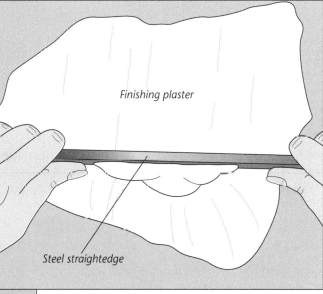

Finishing plaster

Steel straightedge

Finishing trowel

6 ▶ Smoothing the patch

For a smooth finish, dip a finishing trowel in water and, holding the trowel at a slight angle to the wall, draw it down from top to bottom *(left)*. When dry, sand and prime the patch.

TOOLKIT
- Cold chisel
- Ball-peen hammer
- Putty knife
- Diagonal-cutting
  pliers

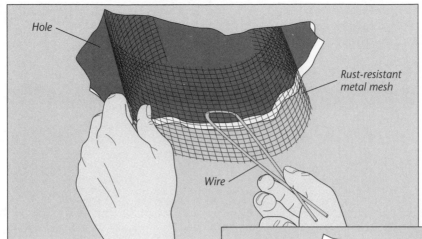

Hole

Rust-resistant
metal mesh

Wire

1 ▶ Preparing the area

After removing loose plaster from around the hole with a cold chisel and a ball-peen hammer, loop a wire through a piece of rust-resistant metal mesh *(left)*. Roll the edges, insert into the hole, and flatten against the back of the damaged surface.

2 ▶ Filling the hole

Tightly wind the wire around a stick. Dampen the hole's edges with a sponge. Using a putty knife, force patching plaster through the mesh *(right)* to fill just over half the hole's depth. Unwind the wire and snip it off with diagonal-cutting pliers. When the plaster is firm, score it to provide "bite" for the next layer. Complete the patch as described on page 61.

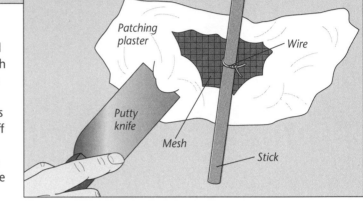

Patching
plaster

Wire

Putty
knife

Mesh

Stick

TILED WALLS

When ceramic tiles become cracked or chipped or work loose from the wall, it's time to replace them. Before you refasten loose tiles, check underneath—a common cause of loosening is moisture under the tiles. Be sure to correct the problem—such as a leaking pipe or roof—and check that the substructure is in good condition.

The directions below for replacing ceramic tiles apply to floors, countertops, and walls. Note that they apply only to tiles installed in a thin-set mastic or mortar-type adhesive, not the thick mortar bed professionals use.

When replacing tiles, choose the right mastic for the area you're tiling. If you're using water-resistant mastic, work in a well-ventilated area. In addition to mastic, you'll need patching plaster to create a base for the new tiles' latex primer, and grout for filling the spaces between tiles. If you don't have any spare replacement tiles, a tile dealer, manufacturer, or contractor may have "bone piles" of old and discontinued tiles where you can find a match. CAUTION: When chipping out old tiles, wear safety goggles to protect your eyes from flying fragments.

**Replacing
a damaged
ceramic tile**

TOOLKIT
- Cold chisel and
  ball-peen hammer
- Glass cutter
- Steel straightedge
- Hammer
- Nailset
- Putty knife
- Paintbrush
  (optional)

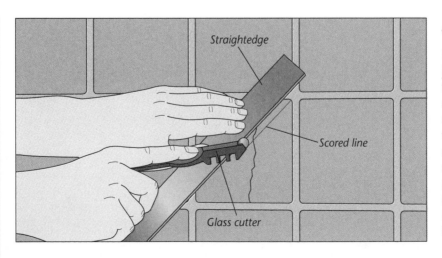

Straightedge

Scored line

Glass cutter

1 ▶ Scoring the tile

Remove grout from the joints around a damaged tile with a cold chisel and ball-peen hammer, unless the joints are wider than $1/8$"—then chip them out when you remove the tile. Using a glass cutter and a steel straightedge, heavily score an X across the tile through the center *(left)*.

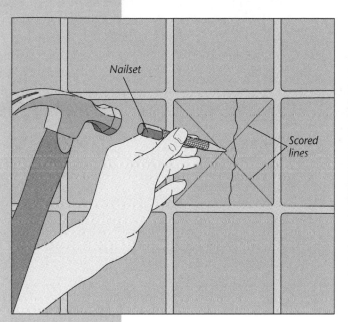

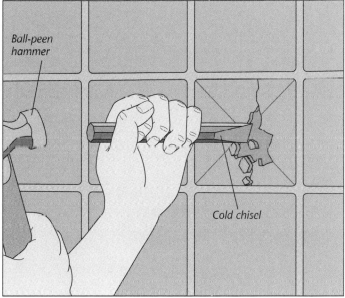

2 Removing the tile

Punch a hole through the center of the damaged tile with a hammer and nailset *(above, left)*. Be careful not to damage the backing. Chip out the tile from the center with a ball-peen hammer and cold chisel using light, rapid blows *(above, right)*.

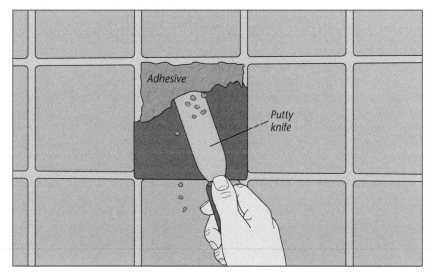

3 Preparing the backing area

Clean the area behind the tile, removing all old adhesive and grout. Use sandpaper to smooth rough spots; dust. Fill the backing with patching plaster, if necessary, to level the backing. When dry, paint with latex primer.

4 Installing a new tile

Apply mastic to the back of the tile with a putty knife when the primer is dry. Keep the mastic 1/2" from the edges. Center the tile and, using a hammer and wood block, gently tap it flush with the surface. Wait 24 hours before grouting.

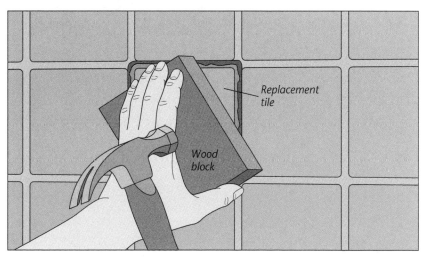

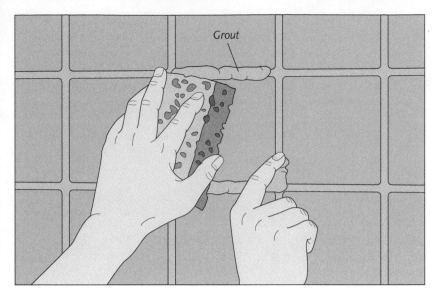

Grout

5 **Grouting**
Fill the joints with grout, using a damp sponge or cloth. Smooth the joints with a wet finger *(left)*. Sponge off any excess grout.

CEILING TILES

Prefabricated ceiling tiles are attached to an existing ceiling or to furring strips, and are secured with staples or nails—with or without adhesive—or adhesive alone.

Often, ceiling tiles show the effect of water damage. To conceal stains or streaks in tiles, apply a primer or clear sealer. When the tiles are dry, you can paint them with latex paint. Another problem you may encounter is dents or chips in tiles. Shown below are the steps to follow in removing and replacing a dented ceiling tile with tongue-and-groove edges.

Replacing a damaged ceiling tile

TOOLKIT
• Utility knife
• Prybar
• Slip-joint pliers
• Putty knife
• Straightedge

1 **Removing the damaged tile**
Cut through all 4 joints *(right)* and pry the tile off its backing; pry out the cut-off tongues from the grooves in the adjacent tiles. Remove remaining staples or nails using slip-joint pliers; scrape off adhesive with a putty knife.

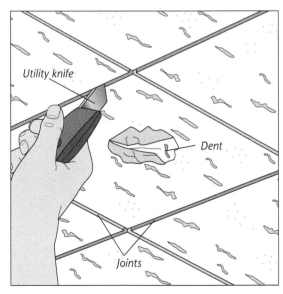

Utility knife

Dent

Joints

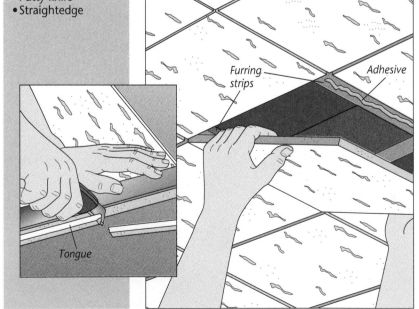

Furring strips

Adhesive

Tongue

2 **Installing a new tile**
Cut the tongue from one edge of the new tile using a utility knife and straightedge *(inset)*. Apply adhesive to the back of the tile or to the furring strips (follow the tile manufacturer's instructions). Position the tile over the opening, slip the remaining tongue into the groove of an adjacent tile *(left)* and press in place until the adhesive holds. You can also use a floor-to-ceiling brace to hold the tile until the adhesive is dry.

FLOORS

A floor consists of finished flooring laid over a sub-floor supported by joists and beams. Joists may have solid or diagonal bridging between them to pro-vide extra strength. The finished floor may be hard-wood or a less expensive softwood, ceramic tile, resilient tile, or sheet flooring. The subfloor may be lumber or plywood panels. In a lumber subfloor, boards are laid diagonally across joists. A plywood subfloor is laid in a staggered fashion with the ends of the panels butted together over the joists and nailed to them. If your house is built on a concrete slab, the floor may be laid over wood sleepers, or laid on a base of plywood.

Flooring problems occur in the surface flooring or are related to defects in the supporting structure. It's important to know how your flooring is attached to the subfloor.

Squeaky floorboards occur when pieces of wood rub together. They can originate in the finished floor, sub-floor, joists, or other parts of the supporting structure due to separations between the joists and subfloor (from drying, inadequate nailing, or settling), weak or loose bridging, and ill-fitting or warped floor boards.

In this section, you'll find repairs for wood flooring (page 66) and resilient tile and sheet flooring (page 68). Repair ceramic tiles as you would wall tiles (page 62).

Silencing squeaky floors from below

TOOLKIT
For angle iron:
• Screwdriver
For screws:
• Drill
• Screwdriver
For a cleat:
• Hammer

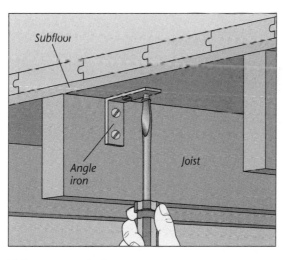

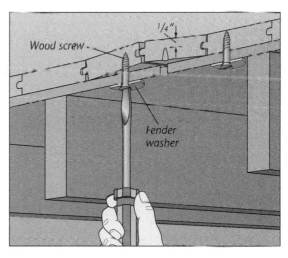

Using an angle iron
Install the angle iron on the joist so the top of it is about 1/4" below the top of the joist. When the angle iron is screwed into the subfloor (above), the floor will be pulled down onto the joist.

Using screws
Drill holes slightly smaller than screw threads; install washers and wood screws, 1/4" shorter than the total floor thickness (above).

Using a cleat
Mount a cleat against a joist under loose boards; prop and tap so the cleat is snug against the subfloor (left). Nail to the joist.

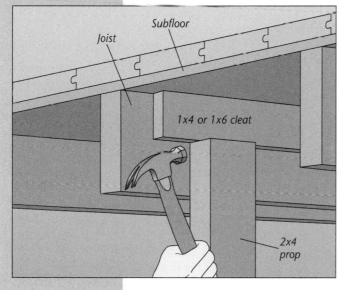

📏 **ASK A PRO**

HOW CAN I LOCATE THE SQUEAK?
In a house where joists are visible from the basement or crawl space, you'll be able to pinpoint squeaks more easily than in homes where joists aren't exposed or where it's an upper floor that's making the noise. If joists are exposed, watch from below while someone walks across the floor above; you may spot movement between joists and sub-floor, or loose bridging between joists. Refer to page 66 for floors over closed-in ceilings or inaccessible spaces.

WOOD FLOORING

Strip and plank flooring are the most common types of wood flooring. They may be milled with square or tongue-and-groove edges and ends, or with a combination of both. Depending on the milling, the boards may be blind-nailed, face-nailed, or screwed to the subfloor *(right)*. Tongue-and-groove strip flooring is almost always blind-nailed; square-edge strip flooring is usually face-nailed. Tongue-and-groove plank flooring may be blind-nailed, screwed or both; square-edged planks may be either face-nailed, screwed, or both. Although plugs are sometimes used just for decoration, they usually indicate that flooring is screwed to the subfloor.

Daily wear and tear causes surface scratches and gouges. The natural expansion and contraction of wood, occurring with changes in temperature or humidity, as well as alternate drying and wetting due to leaks, can cause nails to pull out of the wood, allowing flooring boards to separate, warp, or raise up from the subfloor. The natural settling of a house can cause separations between the joists and the subfloor, too. If your floor is sagging or uneven, there could be a serious structural problem; consult a professional contractor or structural engineer.

You can repair most minor surface damage yourself. Repair split, loose, or warped floorboards as soon as trouble appears. If the damage is extensive, you may

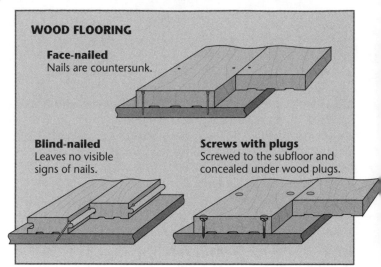

WOOD FLOORING

Face-nailed
Nails are countersunk.

Blind-nailed
Leaves no visible signs of nails.

Screws with plugs
Screwed to the subfloor and concealed under wood plugs.

need to replace boards or sections of flooring. (Replace sections only after determining the methods of milling and securing to the subfloor.) If the overall appearance and condition of your floor are suffering, you may want to make repairs and replacements where necessary and then refinish the entire floor. For refinishing techniques, consult a specialist in wood flooring. When you're refinishing the repaired area, match its color and protective finish as closely as possible to the surrounding area to effectively hide the repair.

 QUICK FIX

SILENCING NOISY FLOORBOARDS
Squirt powdered or liquid graphite between boards or dust cracks with talcum powder. Or apply floor oil to the floor or a few drops of mineral oil between boards (use sparingly). Ill-fitting or warped boards can often be fixed from above. Work wood putty between boards or drill angled pilot holes (right) *through the board into the subfloor, and if possible into a joist. Drive in annular-ring nails, countersink, and fill; the areas where you nail may be conspicuous. If joists are exposed, you can work on the floor from underneath. Toenail loose bridging; tighten other loose areas as shown on page 65.*

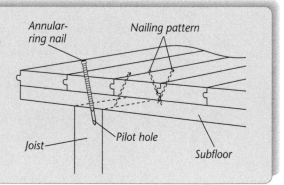

Annular-ring nail

Nailing pattern

Joist

Pilot hole

Subfloor

Repairing surface damage

TOOLKIT

For deep burns:
• Pocketknife

Tackling marks and scratches
Make repairs immediately. You'll probably have to remove the protective finish first and then refinish once the repair has been completed. When using stripping or finishing products, always follow the manufacturer's instructions.

Rub water marks with fine-grade steel wool and a little paste wax or a solvent-base liquid floor wax. If the marks remain, wipe the wax with a soft cloth and rub again with fine-grade steel wool and odorless mineral spirits; wipe clean.

For minor surface burn marks, lightly sand and wipe clean. When dry, finish as desired. For deeper burns, scrape out the burned wood with a sharp knife. Apply one or more coats of scratch hider, putty stick, or stick shellac.

You can conceal a shallow scratch with 1 or 2 applications of scratch hider or crayon. For deep scratches and gouges, fill with matching wood putty, putty stick, or stick shellac. Let dry; then sand smooth with fine-grade sandpaper.

Repairing a split floorboard

TOOLKIT
- Drill
- Nailset
- Hammer

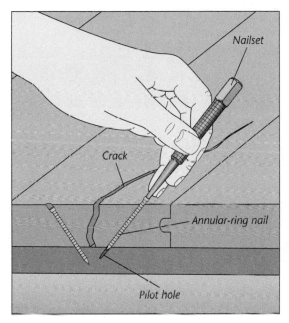

1 ▶ Fastening

Drill angled pilot holes every few inches along the length of the crack. Squirt woodworker's glue into the crack. Drive and countersink annular-ring nails *(left)* into the holes. Wipe off excess glue.

2 ▶ Filling the split

Fill the nail holes and crack with wood putty *(right)*. Sand the putty when it's dry with fine-grade steel wool and finish to match the rest of the floor.

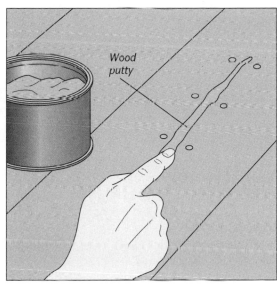

Repairing a loose floorboard

TOOLKIT
- Drill
For repairs from below:
- Screwdriver
For repairs from above:
- Nailset
- Hammer

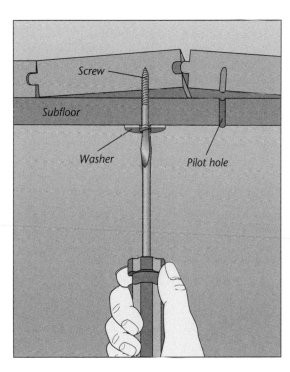

Attaching a floorboard from below

Drill pilot holes through the subfloor and just into the boards; insert screws *(left)*.

Attaching a floorboard from above

Drill pilot holes; drive and countersink annular-ring nails *(right)*, fill with wood putty. Sand the putty when it's dry with fine-grade steel wool and finish to match the rest of the floor.

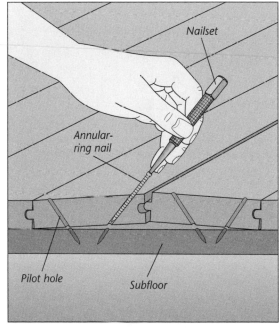

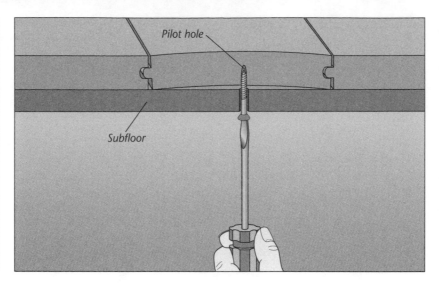

Repairing a warped board

TOOLKIT
• Drill
• Screwdriver

Pilot hole

Subfloor

Wetting and attaching the board
This repair is best done from below, although it can be done from above. Cover the warped board with a damp towel for 48 hours. Drill pilot holes through the subfloor and floorboard every few inches. Insert and tighten screws *(left)*. You may need to refinish the board when the repair is completed.

RESILIENT FLOORING

This family of floor coverings includes linoleum, cork, polyurethane, vinyl, vinyl-asbestos, rubber, and asphalt materials. Resilient flooring is found in individual tiles or in sheets up to 12 feet wide. Both types (in existing floorings) are laid in solvent- or water-base adhesive on concrete, plywood, or hardboard; some tiles are self-sticking. (CAUTION: Flooring materials that contain asbestos are no longer manufactured because they are a proven health hazard. If you are planning to remove, cut, or sand existing floorings installed before 1986, first contact your state health department or EPA office for recommendations.)

Resilient floors are flexible, resistant to moisture and stains, and easy to maintain. Even so, they can get scratched, stained, or gouged, and may develop bumps, bubbles, or curled edges. These minor surface problems may indicate problems in the underlayment or subfloor.

Before you try to repair or replace damaged sections, you'll need to determine the cause of the damage and make the necessary repairs, as described below. Most minor suface repairs can be be carried out using simple tools and techniques. You can either touch up the surface to conceal the flaws, or patch or replace the damaged area. To remove surface stains, refasten curled tiles, or repair bubbles and small holes, see the opposite page. If a tile is badly scratched or gouged, you'll have to take it up and replace it. Sheet flooring can be patched *(page 70)*; take a sample of the flooring to a supplier to get the appropriate adhesive. The supplier will also want to know what kind of underlayment you have.

For all repairs to resilient flooring, you should use a latex water-base adhesive. NOTE: Because of the danger of fire or explosion, the older solvent-base adhesives have largely been replaced by water-base adhesives.

 ASK A PRO

CAN SURFACE DAMAGE POINT TO A MORE SERIOUS PROBLEM?

Generally, the cause of most surface damage in resilient flooring is readily apparent. But some minor surface damage can often be traced to more serious problems in the subfloor or supporting structure. A regular pattern of indentations, running for several feet or forming T's, may be caused by separations in the subfloor due to wood shrinkage or settling of the structure. If you see this, remove the floor covering and have the underlayment and subfloor repaired.

Small bumps in the surface of the floor may be caused by nails that have worked loose. Over time, movement in the structure can cause the subfloor to separate from the joists, forcing the nails up into the resilient flooring. Or, if the origi-

nal flooring was installed when there was too much moisture in the subfloor, the nails may have worked loose as the wood dried. You can place a wood block over the bumps and tap it lightly with a hammer to drive the nail heads flush. If this doesn't work, you'll have to remove the floor covering to gain access to the subfloor.

If tiles have curled at the edge or popped loose in one area, there may be a minor plumbing leak; stop it (page 47) before you fix the flooring. Moisture may cause sheet vinyl to work loose around the perimeter of a room. Moisture in the floors of rooms at or below grade level is often due to poor drainage outside; solve the problem before repairing the flooring.

Fastening a curled tile

TOOLKIT
- Iron
- Putty knife
- Notched spreader

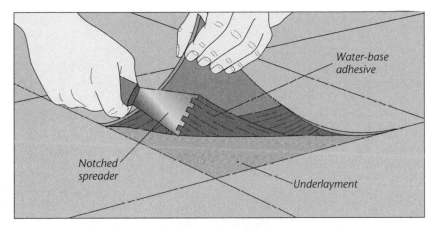

Water-base adhesive

Notched spreader

Underlayment

Regluing the tile
Soften the adhesive with a warm iron; scrape it off the underlayment with a putty knife. Apply water-base adhesive to the tile with a notched spreader *(left)*, press down, and weight overnight.

Flattening a bubble

TOOLKIT
- Iron
- Utility knife
- Putty knife

Cutting and gluing the bubble
Soften the tile with a warm iron; slit the bubble edge to edge with a utility knife. Use a putty knife to force water-base adhesive inside *(right)*. Press flat and weight overnight.

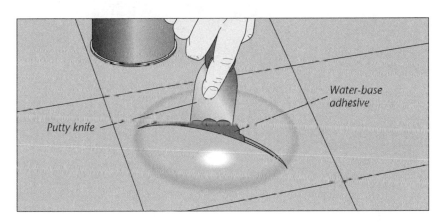

Putty knife

Water-base adhesive

Repairing a small hole or gouge

TOOLKIT
- Putty knife

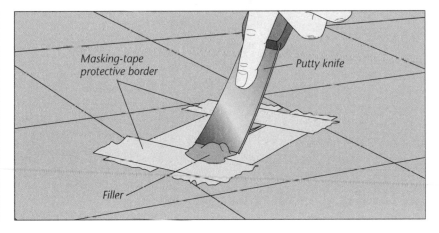

Masking-tape protective border

Putty knife

Filler

Filling the hole
With a putty knife, apply a filler made of fine powder scraped from leftover flooring and a few drops of clear nail polish. Protect the surrounding area with tape *(left)*. Buff with fine-grade steel wool when dry.

 MAINTENANCE TIP

REMOVING STAINS FROM RESILIENT FLOORING

To prevent stains, wipe up spills promptly. For stubborn stains, wipe with a clean cloth moistened with liquid detergent floor cleaner (use a nylon pad for heavy residue). If detergent doesn't remove the stain, try the following products, one at a time, in order: rubbing alcohol, liquid chlorine bleach, turpentine, nail polish remover, and lighter fluid. Do not apply chlorine bleach to cork; turpentine, nail polish remover, or lighter fluid to asphalt or rubber tile; or nail polish remover to vinyl and vinyl-asbestos. Avoid using abrasive scouring powders or pads on resilient flooring. Before using any cleaning product, test it on an inconspicuous area.

Use a clean cloth, turning it frequently. Don't walk on the treated area for 30 minutes. When the stain is gone, rinse the area with water and let it dry; apply floor polish or wax, if it's normally used. Consult your flooring dealer with any other cleaning questions.

Replacing a damaged resilient tile

TOOLKIT
• Propane torch with flame spreader
• Putty knife
• Notched trowel

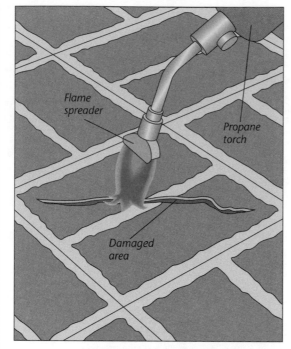

Flame spreader

Propane torch

Damaged area

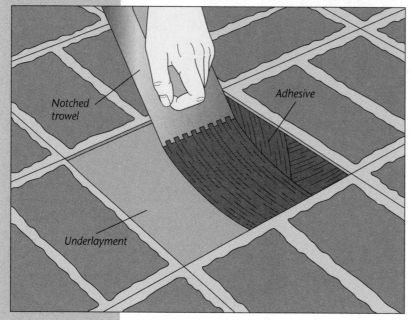

Notched trowel

Adhesive

Underlayment

1 Removing the tile
CAUTION: Keep in mind that old tiles and adhesives may contain asbestos; consult your state health department or EPA office before proceeding with any repairs. To remove a tile, use a propane torch with a flame spreader *(left)* to soften the adhesive under the damaged tile. (The tile should be warm but not too hot to touch.) Pry up a corner of the tile with a putty knife *(below)*; free the tile. Let the adhesive cool and harden (it will take about an hour) before you scrape it away. Check that the underlayment is smooth and flat.

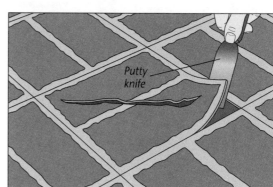

Putty knife

2 Gluing and installing the new tile
Spread a thin, even layer of water-base adhesive on the underlayment using a notched trowel *(left)*, following the adhesive manufacturer's instructions. Make sure you don't get any adhesive on adjacent tiles. Butt two adjoining edges of the new tile against two bordering tiles, matching the pattern, if any. Press the tile in place. Be sure the new tile is level with the adjacent ones. If it's too low, lift it up and apply more adhesive. If it's too high, press it down to squeeze out excess adhesive. Remove any smudges or excess adhesive and let the adhesive dry completely before walking on the floor.

 ASK A PRO

HOW CAN I PATCH SHEET FLOORING?
Using a utility knife, cut a piece of leftover flooring to cover the damaged area. Tape the piece to the floor, matching the pattern. Cut through the patch and old flooring together (right). With a putty knife or old chisel, pry up the old flooring and remove the adhesive. Apply new adhesive on the patch with a notched trowel and press the patch firmly in place, until it's level with the rest of the flooring.

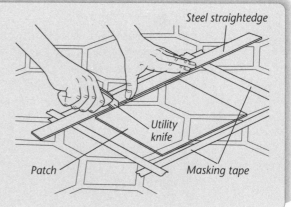

Steel straightedge

Utility knife

Patch

Masking tape

STAIRS

Squeaks in stairs are usually caused by a loose tread rubbing against a riser or the stringers. Treads become loose when joints open due to shrinkage or when supporting blocks or nails work loose.

If squeaks come from where you step, concentrate your repair efforts there. If the noise comes from one side when you step in the center, or if it comes from the rear of the tread when you step at the front, first secure the place where you step, then move to the source of the noise.

If the stairs are accessible from underneath, work on them from below so your repairs won't show. You can use wedges, brackets, or wood blocks to secure the treads to the risers *(page 72)*. If you don't have access from below, you'll have to work from above.

To prevent the wood from splitting, drill pilot holes *(page 73)* before inserting nails or screws; counterbore the holes if you plan to fill them with dowel plugs.

Most wood banisters consist of one or two handrails, balusters, and one or more supporting newel posts. Repeated use can weaken the banister, resulting in loose handrails, balusters, or posts. You can tighten loose parts by inserting wedges or by securing any loose joints with screws. If you're using screws, first counterbore holes. To conceal them, fill the holes with wood putty—colored to match the wood—and sand the putty smooth.

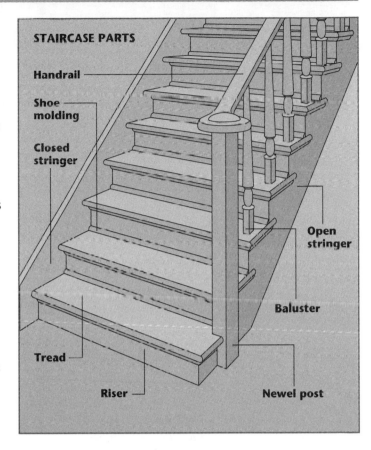

STAIRCASE PARTS

Handrail
Shoe molding
Closed stringer
Open stringer
Baluster
Tread
Riser
Newel post

Fixing squeaky stairs from above

TOOLKIT

For pilot holes with nails:
- Drill
- Hammer
- Nailset
- Putty knife

For pilot holes with screws:
- Drill and combination bit
- Screwdriver bit or screwdriver

For wedges:
- Butt chisel
- Hammer
- Utility knife

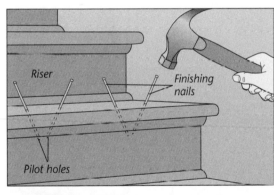

Riser
Finishing nails
Pilot holes

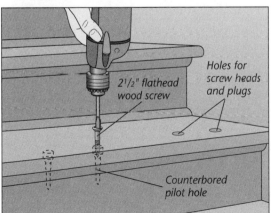

2½" flathead wood screw
Holes for screw heads and plugs
Counterbored pilot hole

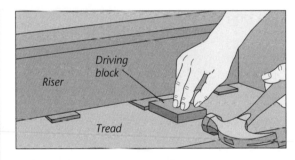

Driving block
Riser
Tread

Using nails, screws or wedges

First, lubricate the stairs by blowing powdered graphite or talcum powder into the joints, especially where the backs of the treads meet the risers. If this doesn't help, try one of the following repairs: Drive and sink nails into angled pilot holes drilled through the tread into the riser *(left, above)*. Use a nailset, then cover with wood putty. You can also drill counterbored pilot holes through the tread into the riser *(left, below)*. Insert screws and glue in dowel plugs.

A third method uses wedges. Before you drive them in, use a butt chisel to remove any shoe molding. Tap in glue-coated wedges between the tread and riser with a hammer *(above)*. Cut them flush with the riser, using a chisel or utility knife, and replace the molding to conceal them.

Fixing stair squeaks from below

TOOLKIT
For wedges:
• Hammer
For brackets:
• Screwdriver
For blocks:
• Drill
• Screwdriver

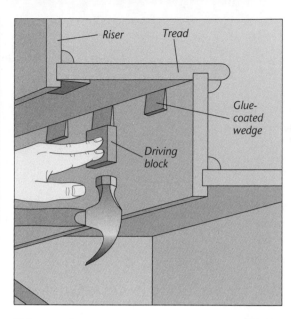

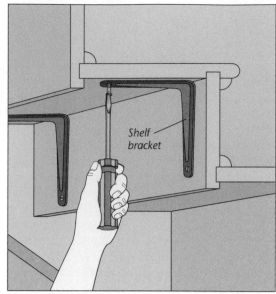

Using wedges, brackets, or blocks
One way to stop squeaks is to tap glue-coated wedges between the tread and riser, using a hammer and driving block *(above, left)*. Or, you can screw brackets under the tread and riser *(above, right)*. If you're using wood blocks to stop a squeak, glue and screw the blocks under the tread and against the riser, keeping the screw ends at least ¼" beneath the surface *(right)*. The inset shows how the pilot holes should be drilled.

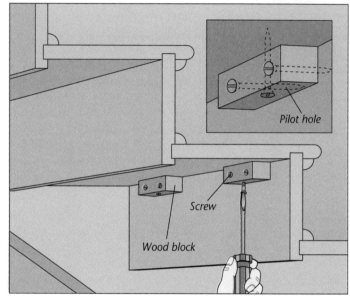

Tightening a loose handrail

TOOLKIT
For wedges:
• Hammer
• Utility knife
For screws:
• Drill and combination bit
• Screwdriver
• Putty knife
• Sanding block
• Paintbrush

Using a wedge
With a hammer, tap a glue-coated wedge between the handrail and baluster *(right)*. Don't pry up the hand-rail as you install the wedge. Using a utility knife, trim the wedge flush with the baluster.

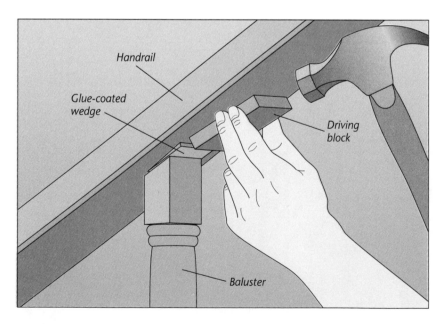

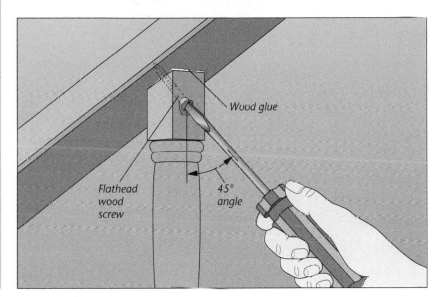

Using a screw
Drill an angled pilot hole through the baluster and into the handrail; countersink the hole. Apply wood glue; insert screw and tighten (*left*). Fill the hole, sand, and then finish.

ASK A PRO

HOW DO I DRILL A PILOT HOLE?

To prevent wood from splitting when joining two pieces of wood together, first drill a body hole through the first piece of wood, using a bit the same size as the diameter of the unthreaded part of the screw. Then use a bit slightly narrower than the screw's threaded part to drill to the full depth of the screw in the second piece of wood. In some situations, you may want to drive the screw's head flush with the surface (countersink) or hide the screw's head and cover it with a wood plug or putty (counterbore). For this, you can either use a special combination bit that drills pilot, body, countersink, and counterbore holes in one operation (you can set the bit to stop at the countersinking stage), or, you can use a selection of bits—always bore the larger hole first and then add the body and pilot holes in the center.

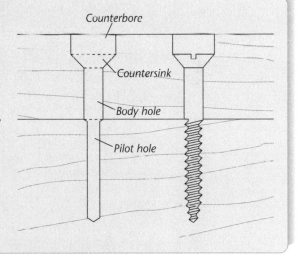

Tightening a loose baluster: type nailed to treads

TOOLKIT
- Drill and combination bit
- Screwdriver
- Putty knife
- Sanding block
- Paintbrush

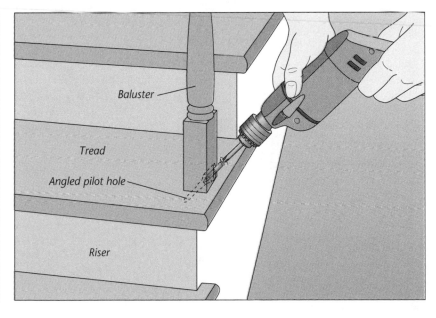

Baluster

Tread

Angled pilot hole

Riser

Using a screw
Drill an angled pilot hole through the baluster and into the tread; countersink the hole. NOTE: A Phillips-head bit and screw are easier to use when you're power-driving. Insert a wood screw and tighten (*left*). Fill the hole with wood putty, sand smooth when dry, and finish.

Tightening a loose baluster: notch-and-tenon type

TOOLKIT
- Putty knife or butt chisel
- Drill and combination bit
- Screwdriver
- Hammer

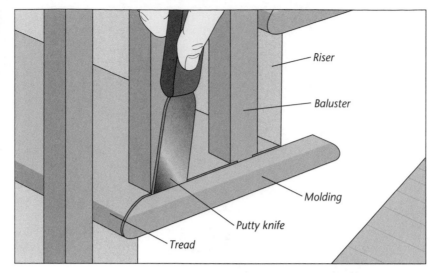

1 Removing the molding
Pry off the molding with a putty knife or butt chisel *(left)*.

Riser

Baluster

Molding

Putty knife

Tread

2 Fastening the baluster
Drill a pilot hole through the tenon and into the tread; countersink the hole. Apply wood glue around the notch and tenon. Insert a wood screw and tighten *(right)*. Replace the molding.

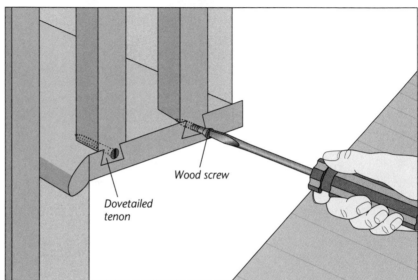

Wood screw

Dovetailed tenon

Tightening a loose newel post

TOOLKIT
- Drill and combination bit
- Screwdriver
- Putty knife
- Sanding block
- Paintbrush

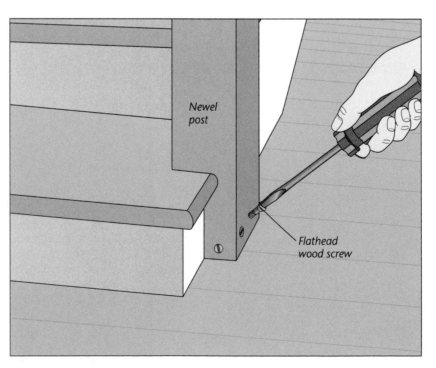

Newel post

Flathead wood screw

Using screws
Drill angled pilot holes near the base of the newel post through the post and into the floor; countersink the holes. Apply wood glue between the post and floor; insert flathead wood screws and tighten *(left)*. Fill the holes with wood putty, sand smooth when dry, and finish.

DOORS

At some point, every homeowner will be faced with the challenge of repairing a binding door or a stiff lock. As the house shifts and wood swells or shrinks with changes in weather, hinged doors will often warp or shift in their frame; by adjusting shims or by planing off a small amount of wood, you may avoid having to replace the door. Instructions for repairing hinged doors begin below. Locksets often need to be lubricated; in some cases they need to be replaced, which can be done easily (*page 80*). Sliding doors (*page 83*) and garage doors (*page 86*) may begin to stick; adjustments to the guides and hinges can solve this problem.

HINGED DOORS

All hinged doors have the same basic framework, sometimes hidden under a solid veneer, consisting of two stiles, running vertically, and two or more rails, running horizontally. The hinges are on one stile; the latch and lock are on the other. The door is hinged to a frame, consisting of jambs, casing, stops, sill, and threshold. The edge of the lock stile is beveled slightly (*right, inset*), so the door can close. The jambs form the sides and head of the frame; the casing acts as trim and as support for the jambs. The stops are wood strips the door fits against when closed. In exterior doors, a sill fits between the jambs, forming the frame bottom. The threshold, or saddle, is fastened to the sill.

Age and use can cause even a well-fitted door to loosen, bind, or warp. The information that follows gives solutions for the most common door problems. If you're working on just one hinge at a time or on the top of a door, you need only open the door partially and drive a wedge underneath the latch side to hold the door steady. But for other repairs, such as sanding or planing the side or bottom of a door, you'll need to remove it from its hinges (*page 77*).

Loose doors: If a door is too small for its frame, you can install weather stripping. If a loose door is causing latch problems, adjust the strike plate (*page 79*).

Binding doors: Binding or sticking can result from a buildup of dirt and paint or from a door that has swelled so that it no longer fits in its frame. Identify the spots that bind by inserting a thin strip of cardboard or wood between the door and jambs. If the door only binds slightly, remove dirt and chisel off large globs of paint on the door edges or jambs; sand the surface. Coat the door edges and jambs with paraffin.

Often, simply tightening loose hinges gets a sagging door back into alignment. Clean

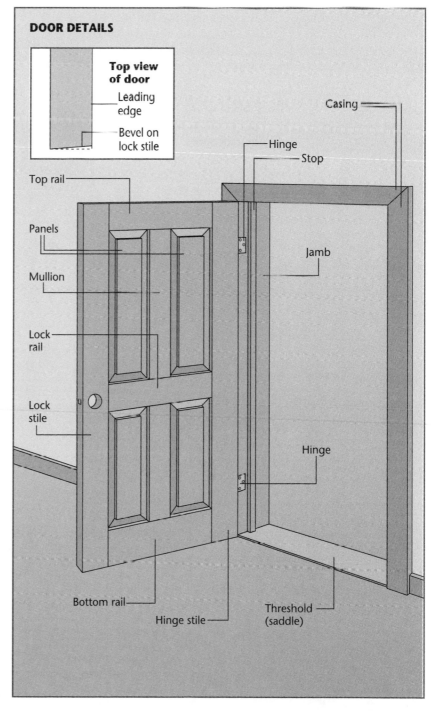

DOOR DETAILS

Top view of door
Leading edge
Bevel on lock stile

Casing

Hinge
Stop

Top rail

Panels

Jamb

Mullion

Lock rail

Lock stile

Hinge

Bottom rail
Hinge stile
Threshold (saddle)

off any dirt and repair or replace any bent hinges. Tighten loose hinge screws; if they can't be tightened, remove them and, one at a time, squirt a little glue in the holes and then fill the hole with match sticks or pieces of wooden dowel and drive screws back in.

If the door binds badly or isn't square in its frame, you may need to shim the hinges or sand or plane the door (if you only need to remove a small amount of wood, sanding is best). See below to help you figure out what repairs are necessary for a binding door.

Warped doors: Avoid warping by sealing the door on all surfaces. If there's a slight bow on the hinge side, center a third hinge between the top and bottom ones to pull the door into alignment. If the bow is near the lock side and the door latches only when slammed, adjust the strike plate *(page 79)*. If this doesn't help, remove and reposition the stop as for a window *(page 89)*. If the top or bottom of the door doesn't meet the stop on the lock side, reposition the stop and the strike plate. You may have to shim the hinges to change the angle of the door's swing. A badly warped door should be replaced.

Latch problems: When a latch won't work, the trouble may be the alignment between the latch and strike plate *(page 79)*. For lockset problems, refer to page 80.

 QUICK FIX

QUIETING SQUEAKY HINGES
Silence a noisy hinge by coating it with silicone spray or light penetrating oil. If the squeak persists, remove the pin and thoroughly clean the pin, barrel, and hinge leaves with steel wool. Coat them lightly with silicone spray or light penetrating oil and replace the pin.

Diagnosing a binding door

Door binding at the top or bottom of the lock side
Reseat the upper hinge and shim out the lower one if the door binds as in (A). Reverse the procedure if it binds as in (B). To reseat the hinge, repair the screw holes and tighten the screws. As a last resort, you can deepen the mortise with a chisel, but getting the right depth can be tricky.

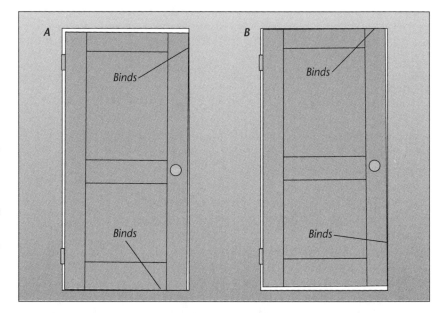

Door binding on the hinge or lock side
For the hinge side (A), remove the door and shim out both hinges, or sand or plane the hinge side. For a door that binds on the lock side (B), sand or plane the hinge side as well and, if necessary, deepen the mortises for the hinges (avoid planing the lock side because it means maintaining the beveled edge along that side).

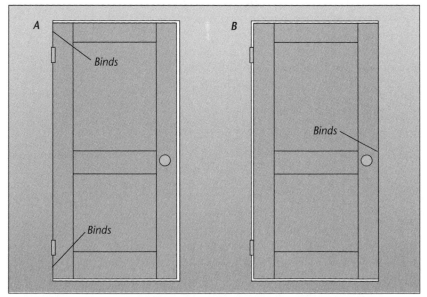

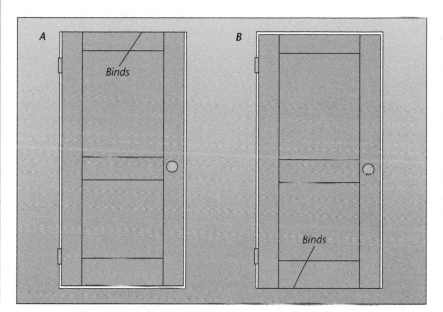

Door binding along the top or bottom

For a door that binds at the top (A), wedge the door open and sand or plane the wood along the top. For one that binds at the bottom (B), remove the door and sand or plane the wood along the bottom. Be careful not to remove too much wood.

Removing and planing a door

TOOLKIT
- Hammer
- Nailset (optional)
- Bench plane
For planing the hinge side:
- Utility knife
- Screwdriver
- Butt chisel

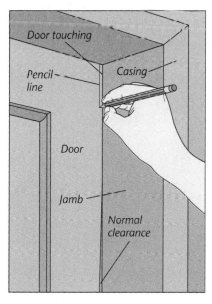

1 Marking

Carefully mark the area to be planed on both faces of the door before removing it. You'll need to keep a close eye on your marks as you plane.

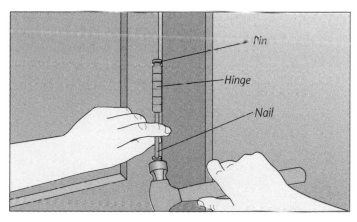

2 Removing the door and hinges

To remove the hinge pins, close the door securely (place a wedge under it or have a helper hold the door). Using a hammer and a nail or nailset, gently tap on the bottom of the lowest pin *(above)* or on the underside of its head to drive it up and out of the hinge barrel. Remove the middle pin, if any, then remove the top pin. Lift the door off its hinges.

If you are going to plane the hinge side, first remove the hinge leaves. Use a utility knife to cut through any paint around the leaves; then unscrew and remove the hinges. After you plane, deepen the hinge mortises with a butt chisel.

 ASK A PRO

HOW DO I SUPPORT A DOOR WHILE I PLANE IT?

One way is to set it on edge and wedge one end into a corner of the room. A better method is to build two door jacks (right), using 1/2-inch plywood or hardboard and 6-inch-long 2x4 blocks. The door's weight will bend the plywood strip and press the blocks together, holding the door. Protect the surface of the door with pieces of cardboard.

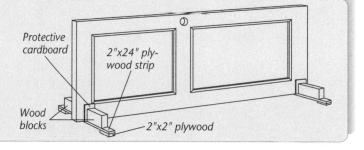

3 Using a plane

Choose a bench plane that's long enough to ensure flat cuts. These planes are available in different sizes—a jack plane type (14" to 15" long) is preferable, but a 9" to 10" smoothing plane type will do the job. The blade should be wider than the thickness of the door so the cuts will be level. Adjust the blade to make paper-thin cuts so you don't remove too much wood.

To avoid gouging the wood, plane in line with the grain. Use two hands, gripping the rear handle with one hand, the front knob or one edge with the other. At the beginning of the cut, apply slightly more pressure on the plane's toe; even out the pressure as you continue the stroke; then, near the end, gradually switch pressure to the heel.

4 Planing the door to fit

Plane the stile, using long strokes with the plane parallel to the stile *(right)*; cut with the grain. Plane the top or bottom of the door by cutting from the ends toward the center *(below)*; this will avoid splitting the ends of the stiles.

To replace the door, start the top pin through the barrel and then position the door. Insert the middle and bottom pins. Wiggle the door until the pins slip in. Leave the pins a little loose so they'll be easier to remove for future repairs.

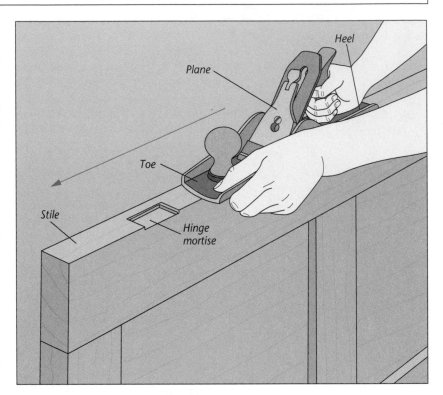

Heel
Plane
Toe
Stile
Hinge mortise

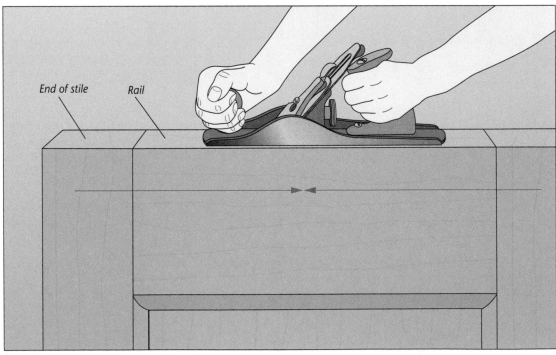

End of stile
Rail

Adjusting a warped door

TOOLKIT
- Screwdriver
OR
- Utility knife
- Butt chisel
- Nail claw
- Hammer

Shimming the hinges
For a door that is warped at the top or bottom, shim the hinges to change the angle of the door's swing. Remove the hinge and place a half-shim under each hinge leaf either on the side of leaf that's closest to the pin, as shown at right, or on the opposite side (depending on the warp). The other hinge is usually shimmed in the opposite way.

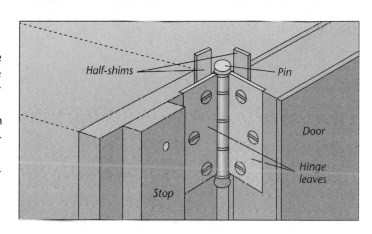

Half-shims — Pin — Door — Hinge leaves — Stop

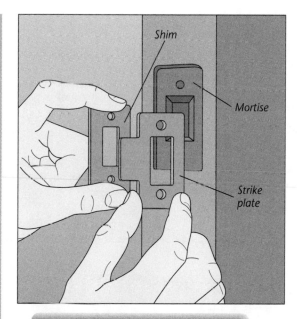

Jamb — Stop — Carboard shim — Nails — Door

Repositioning the stop
This works best if the warp is near the latch (the door latches only if slammed hard), and if the warp is too much for shimming to correct. First use a sharp knife to score the paint between the stop and the door frame. Starting at the bottom, use a wide chisel to pry off the stop. Remove the nails, close the door, and prop the stop against the door. Insert a thin cardboard shim between stop and door. Pressing the stop against the shim, nail the stop into place using 2" finishing nails. For an exterior door, repaint the stop to weatherproof the joint. If this resetting of the stop moves it much more than $1/16$", you may also need to shim the hinges as described above.

Adjusting a strike plate

TOOLKIT
- Screwdriver
To enlarge strike plate opening:
- File
To enlarge mortise:
- Butt chisel
- Mallet or hammer
- Putty knife

Shim — Mortise — Strike plate

Diagnosing and solving the problem
If a door latch doesn't catch, close the door and watch how the latch bolt meets the strike plate; also, scars on the strike plate's surface indicate the degree and direction of misalignment. Or, the door may have shrunk and the latch can't reach the strike plate.

If the door has warped slightly, adjust it as explained above; otherwise adjust the strike plate. For less than a $1/8$" misalignment, remove the strike plate and file its inside edge to enlarge the opening. For more than a $1/8$" misalignment, remove the strike plate and, with a butt chisel, extend the mortise higher or lower as needed. Replace the plate, fill the gap at top or bottom with wood putty, and refinish. If the latch doesn't reach the strike plate, shim out the plate *(left)* or add another strike plate. If the latch still won't reach, shim out the door's hinges.

 ASK A PRO

HOW DO I MAKE A SHIM?
To make a shim for a door hinge or strike plate, use thin sheet brass (available in several thicknesses) or dense, hard-surfaced cardboard (such as that used in file folders). Use the hinge leaf or strike plate as a pattern; the shim should be minutely smaller in each dimension. Cut the shim and make the screw holes. Don't glue the shim in place—you may want to remove it later on.

REPAIRING AND REPLACING LOCKSETS

Most locksets for doors fall into two categories. One type, encompassing both cylindrical and tubular locksets, fits into a hole bored in the door's face (the tubular lockset is simpler than the cylindrical, and has smaller locking mechanisms). The other type, a mortise lockset, fits into a large recess cut into the edge of the door. The lockset has one or two lock buttons in the face plate and usually a deadbolt that double-locks the door, as well as a spring-loaded thumb latch on the exterior handle.

Consult the chart below for solutions to a range of common lock problems; if a door doesn't latch, realign it or the strike plate *(page 79)*. If your problem requires professional help, remove the lock and take it to a locksmith—less expensive than a house call.

Often, it's simpler to replace the lockset *(below)* than to try to fix it. Replace it with the same type; take the old lockset to the store with you. (Mortise locksets for interior doors may be hard to find, however.)

 QUICK FIX

TIGHTENING A LOOSE DOORKNOB

Often, the doorknobs of old-fashioned mortise locksets become loose. To tighten, loosen the screw on the knob's shank as shown on page 82. Hold the knob on the other side of the door tight and turn the loose one clockwise until it fits snugly against the rose. Then tighten the screw until you feel it resting against a flat side of the spindle. The knob should turn freely. If this doesn't help, remove the knob and check the spindle; if it's worn, replace it.

TROUBLESHOOTING A PROBLEM LOCKSET

Problem:	It may be...	Try this:
Latch sticks or responds slowly	Gummed up or dirty lock mechanism	Blow a pinch of powdered graphite or pencil lead into lock mechanism or keyway, or inject light penetrating oil or silicone spray into lock mechanism
Key doesn't insert smoothly	Dirty keyway and tumbler area	Blow a pinch of graphite or pencil lead or spray silicone spray into keyway (don't use oil)
	Foreign object in keyway	Attempt to dislodge object with thin, stiff wire
Key doesn't insert at all	Ice in keyway	Chip ice from opening; carefully heat key with a match; then insert key in lock and work it gently until ice melts
Key is broken in lock	Improperly inserted key, ill-fitting replacement key, or wrong key forced into lock	Remove broken key with thin, stiff hooked wire or with coping saw blade; if this doesn't work, remove lock cylinder and push key fragment out from other side with thin, stiff wire
Key won't turn in lock	Cylinder turned in faceplate	Move cylinder to proper position
	Poorly duplicated key	Check key against original; replace if necessary
	Damaged tumblers	Replace cylinder or entire lockset
Key turns but doesn't operate locking mechanism	Broken lock mechanism	Repair or replace lockset

Replacing a cylindrical lockset

TOOLKIT
• Screwdriver

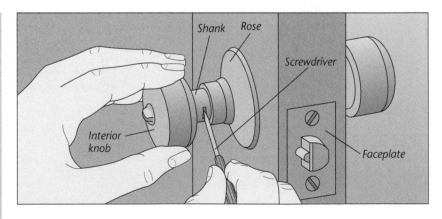

1 Removing the interior handle
To release the interior knob, push the tip of a small screwdriver into the slot on the shank *(left)*, or insert a nail into the hole, or push the shank button if there is one. Snap off the rose.

2 ▶ Removing the cylinder

Unscrew and remove the mounting plate *(right)*; slip out the exterior knob and cylinder. Unscrew and remove the faceplate and latch assembly. Remove the strike plate from the door jamb.

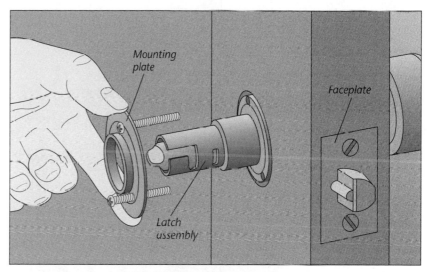

Mounting plate

Faceplate

Latch assembly

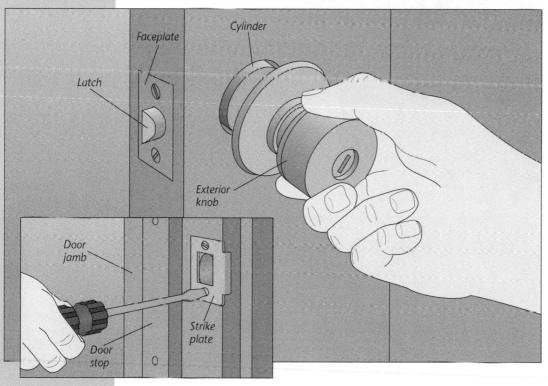

Faceplate

Cylinder

Latch

Exterior knob

Door jamb

Strike plate

Door stop

3 ◀ Installing the new lockset

Insert and screw on the new latch assembly and face plate. Holding the exterior knob and cylinder, slide the cylinder in *(left)* and engage it with the latch assembly. Attach the mounting plate; snap on the interior rose and knob. Screw on the new strike plate *(inset)* and make sure that the latch engages in the strike plate.

 ASK A PRO

HOW DO I DRILL THE HOLES FOR A NEW LOCKSET?

A template and instructions should be included with your lockset. Place the knob 36 to 38 inches above the floor. Always bore the lock hole first, using a hole saw: As soon as the guide bit on the hole saw exits the opposite side of the door, stop and continue from the other side. This will help prevent tearout when the hole saw exits. Use a spade bit to bore the latch hole, as shown. Next, close the door and mark the top and bottom of the latch where it contacts the jamb. Position the strike plate there; chisel out a mortise for the latch.

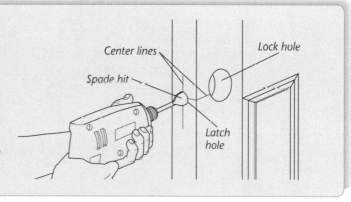

Center lines

Lock hole

Spade bit

Latch hole

Replacing a mortise lockset

TOOLKIT
• Screwdriver

1 ▶ Removing the old hardware

Remove the interior knob and deadbolt knob by loosening the screw at the base of each *(right)*. Unscrew and remove the exterior handle, and any trim. Remove the spindle (a two-piece type will have to be unhooked in the middle).

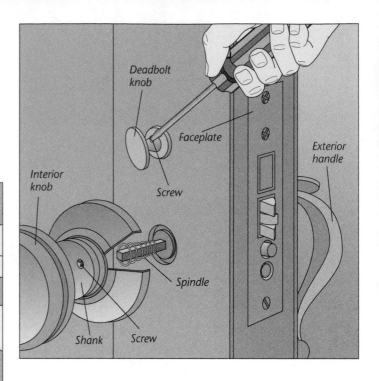

Deadbolt knob
Faceplate
Interior knob
Exterior handle
Screw
Spindle
Shank
Screw

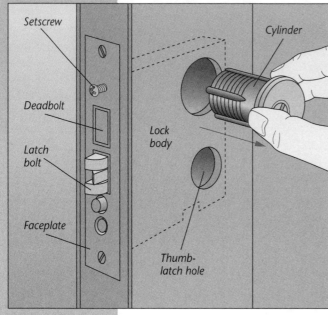

Setscrew
Cylinder
Deadbolt
Lock body
Latch bolt
Faceplate
Thumb-latch hole

2 ◀ Removing the cylinder

On the faceplate, loosen the setscrew opposite the cylinder. Unscrew and remove the cylinder *(left)*. Unscrew the faceplate and remove the lock body.

3 ◀ Installing the new lockset

Slip the new lock body into the recess in the door *(left)* and fasten the faceplate so it is flush with the door edge. Install the cylinder; then mount the exterior handle, deadbolt knob, and interior knob.

Install the strike plate so it sits flush with the jamb edge *(inset)*. Make sure that the latch bolt and the deadbolt engage the strike plate correctly; make any necessary adjustments. Finally, install any decorative trim.

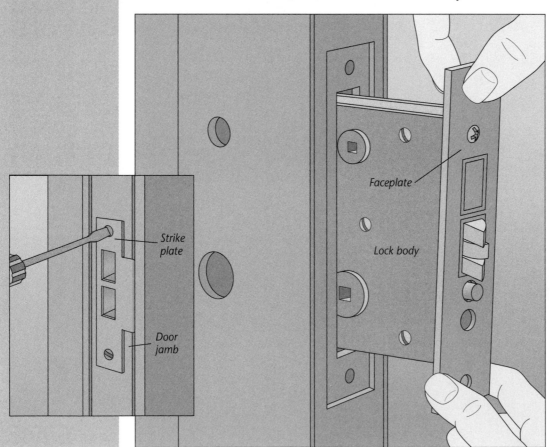

Strike plate
Door jamb
Faceplate
Lock body

SLIDING DOORS

All sliding doors operate in one of two ways, though the variety of their hardware is almost unlimited. Some lightweight sliding doors, such as closet doors and pocket doors (which slide into walls), as well as extremely heavy garage doors, are hung from the top rail. Moderately heavy doors, such as patio doors, usually rest on the bottom rail. Nearly all sliding doors glide on rollers. These can be adjusted to make the door ride either higher or lower. Plastic guides at the top or bottom keep the doors vertical and aligned with their tracks.

Inspect all hardware periodically. Tighten any loosened screws in the frame or track and replace any part that's worn, broken, or missing. Removing a sliding door for maintenance or repair is simple (below) but keep in mind that the door can be very heavy, especially if it is made from glass.

All tracks, especially the one that supports the rollers must be kept free of foreign objects and dirt so the door doesn't bind. Occasional application of a little powdered graphite or paraffin to the track helps keep the operation smooth and quiet. If your door has metal wheels, a drop of oil to each roller bearing will also help; nylon wheels shouldn't be oiled.

If a sliding door jumps off its track, check for a dirty track, a section that has been bent out of shape, or a guide that has come out of alignment. A door that drags or is tilted in its frame usually needs roller adjustment. (There should be a ⅜-inch clearance between the bottom of the door and the floor or rug.) You can also compensate for a minor warp in a door by adjusting the rollers. However, if you have a sliding door that is seriously warped, you'll need to replace it.

Removing a sliding door

Lifting out a bottom-supported door
Lift a bottom-supported door straight up to clear the track; to remove it, sharply angle the lower part of the door outward (right). You may need a helper to hold the door, since it can be heavy.

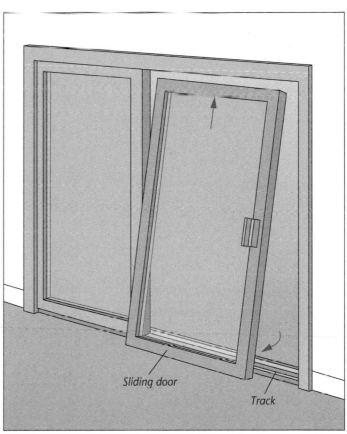

Sliding door

Track

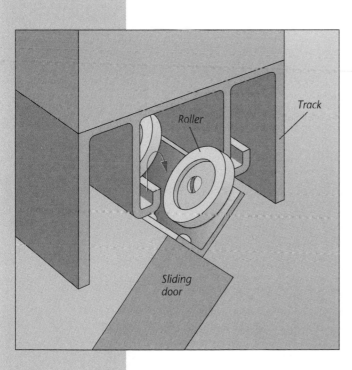

Track

Roller

Sliding door

Lifting out a top-hung door
Lift a top-hung door straight up and angle it so that you can lift the rollers out of the track (left). (Some top-hung doors have notches on the track that you must align with the rollers before you can lift the door out.)

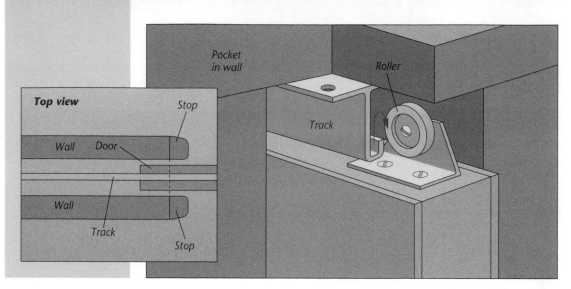

Top view

Wall   Door   Stop

Wall

Track   Stop

Pocket in wall

Roller

Track

Lifting out a pocket door

Some pocket doors have a quick-release mechanism. If your door doesn't have one, remove both stops from the head jamb and one side jamb stop to allow the door to swing out. To remove the door, angle the bottom out and then lift the door up and over the track.

Fixing track and guide problems

TOOLKIT
• Hammer for straightening track
• Screwdriver for straightening guides

Straightening the track

If part of the track is bent, put a block of wood in it of about the same width as the track. With a hammer, tap at the bent section to straighten it against the block of wood.

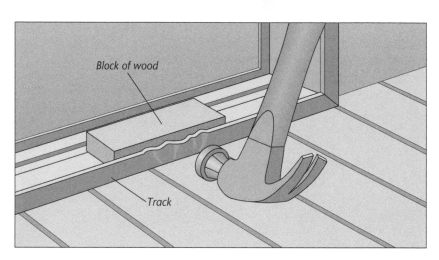

Block of wood

Track

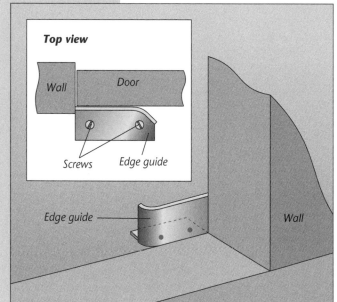

Top view

Wall   Door

Screws   Edge guide

Edge guide

Wall

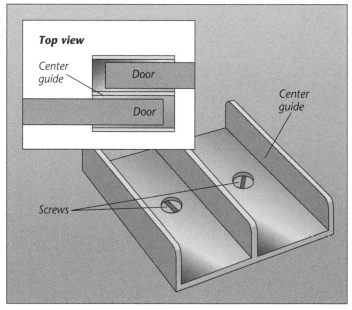

Top view

Center guide   Door

Door

Center guide

Screws

Aligning guides

If a top-hung door binds, check the alignment of the guides on the floor. There is likely one at the edge of the wall at each end of the doorway (above, left), and one near the middle of the doorway (above, right). Unscrew and reposition the problem guide so the door doesn't catch on it.

TOOLKIT
• Screwdriver

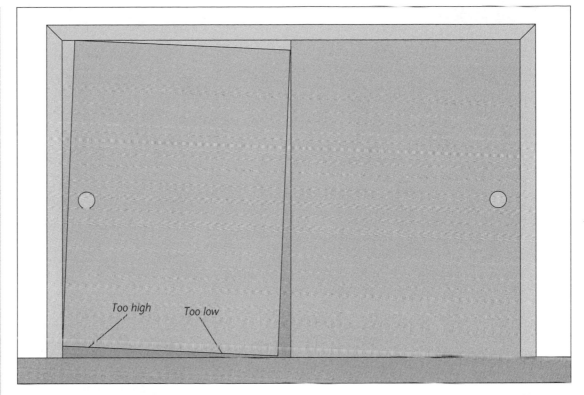

Diagnosing the problem

If a door drags or is visibly tilted *(above)*, the rollers need adjustment or replacement. If the wheels are obviously worn or broken, replace them. It can be difficult to find replacement wheels for many doors —take the broken part and as much information about the door as you can to a dealer. If the wheels are in good shape, adjust them. The best approach is to adjust all wheels to their fully retracted position, then to proceed to align the door and set the clearances by measurement.

Adjusting a bottom-supported door

In a bottom-supported door, there's an adjusting screw inside a hole near the bottom edge of the door at each end. Insert a screwdriver into the hole and turn the screw to move the rollers *(left)*. Lower the rollers to push that corner of the door up, or raise them to drop that corner down.

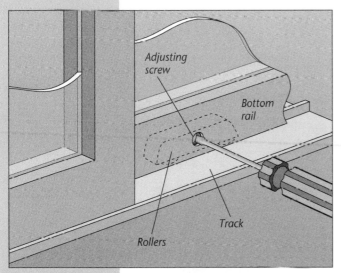

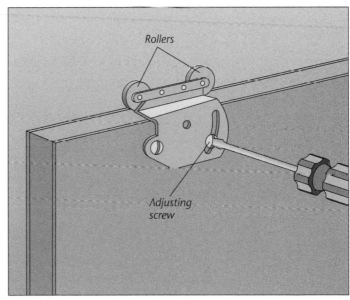

Adjusting a top-hung door

Adjust the height of the roller at each end of the door. To raise a corner of the door, loosen the adjusting screw on the roller at that corner *(right)*; move it lower to pull the door up. To lower a corner of the door, raise the rollers at that corner.

GARAGE DOORS

The most common type of garage door is the roll-up, or sectional, door. This type of door has either two tension springs, one at each side of the door, as shown at right, or a single torsion spring that extends across the top of the garage-door opening. There are also swing-up, or one-piece, doors. These pivot on hinges and usually have springs on each side to adjust the balance.

Regular maintenance will head off many problems. Periodically clean the tracks and lubricate them with penetrating oil or silicone spray. Tighten the screws on the hardware, and clean and lubricate the hinges and rollers. Use powdered graphite on the lock. Keep the door sealed and painted to prevent moisture damage.

A garage door may bind or drag because of poor roller and track alignment, broken rollers, or loose hinges. If the door won't stay up or down, an adjustment of the tension may be necessary.

Electric door openers should have a return switch so the door will reverse automatically when it meets an obstacle. If the door doesn't open or close completely, won't stay open, or won't reverse, you can make adjustments to the electric door opener following the manufacturer's instructions. CAUTION: Always test the door carefully after the adjustment.

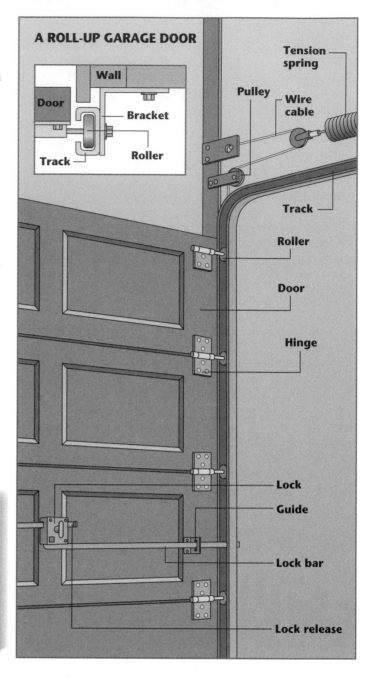

A ROLL-UP GARAGE DOOR

Wall · Door · Bracket · Track · Roller

Tension spring · Pulley · Wire cable · Track · Roller · Door · Hinge · Lock · Guide · Lock bar · Lock release

PLAY IT SAFE

MAINTAINING AND REPLACING TENSION SPRINGS
Inspect the tension springs regularly and get any replaced if they are developing bulges or are unevenly spaced. Adjusting or replacing the tension springs on a roll-up door or the springs of a swing-up door is a dangerous job best left to a professional. (You can, however, adjust the cable as shown opposite). Have safety cables installed in the springs if they're not already in place.

Adjusting a dragging or binding door

TOOLKIT
• Adjustable wrench
For aligning tracks:
• Hammer or mallet

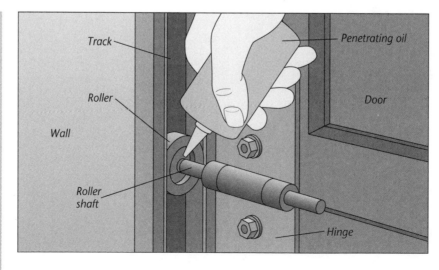

Track · Roller · Wall · Roller shaft · Penetrating oil · Door · Hinge

Repairing hinges and rollers
If the rollers bind, the cause could be bent or loose hinges, or broken rollers. Tighten loose hinges; repair bent ones. Replace broken rollers and lubricate them with penetrating oil *(left)*.

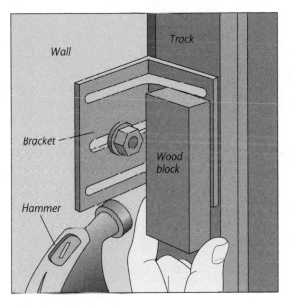

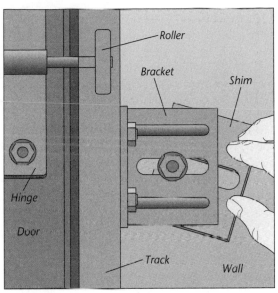

Aligning tracks

If the door drags, the tracks may be out of alignment. Loosen the brackets and tap the track with a hammer and wood block *(above)*, or with a mallet, until it's aligned; then tighten the brackets.

Adjusting rollers

If the door binds due to rollers that are improperly positioned or set too deep, adjust the placement of the brackets. In some cases the brackets may need to be shimmed out *(above)*.

Adjusting the lock bar

TOOLKIT
• Screwdriver

Moving the guide

If the lock bar doesn't align with the slot in the track, loosen the screws in the guide and move it up or down until the lock bar catches *(right)*. Tighten the screws.

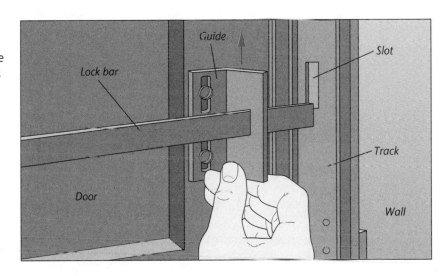

Adjusting the tension

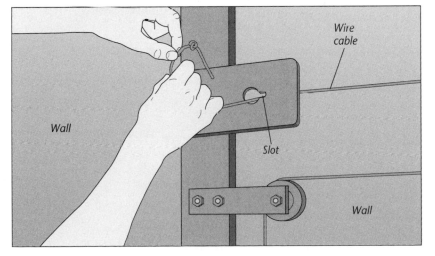

Tightening the tension wire

You can adjust the tension on a roll-up door by pulling on the wire cable *(left)* to take up the slack (the door should be in the open position). Knot the cable end to secure it in the slot.

WINDOWS

In this section, we'll look at repairs for double-hung windows *(below)*, casement windows *(page 92)*, and sliding windows *(page 93)*.

Weather stripping on windows helps to keep out cold drafts in winter. Most windows are weather-stripped at the factory, but older windows may not be. You can install weather stripping yourself. Three types are avail-able: spring-type, which is better suited to double-hung windows; pliable gasket, which is ideal for wood case-ment windows and sliding doors with wood sashes; and compressible felt strip, which is less durable, but can be used where a warped window doesn't close tightly. Follow manufacturer's instructions, and consult your local home improvement center with any questions.

DOUBLE-HUNG WINDOWS

A double-hung window *(right)* consists of two sashes: an upper, outside sash that moves down and a lower, inside one that moves up. A pulley and weight system or balances located in the jambs control the movement of the sashes. Double-hung windows may be made from wood, aluminum, or vinyl. The latter types seldom require repairs. To keep them operating smoothly, occasionally clean the channels with very fine steel wool and coat them with silicone spray.

As a wood window sash ages, it may begin to misfit its frame, or else the system that controls sash movement may break down. Refer to page 90 for instructions on remov-ing wood sashes and replacing a window's balance system.

If a sash is temporarily stuck because moisture has swelled the wood, a change of weather may correct it. If the sash is too wide, sand it down or, in severe cases, plane it. Check constantly for fit: sanding too much can result in a loose sash. This will let in unwanted air, which weather stripping can correct.

Replacing a window pane isn't difficult. However, insulated or safety glass must be replaced by a glazier. For metal sashes, glass may be held in place by rubber seals, a rub-ber gasket, or beveled metal or plastic snap-out moldings.

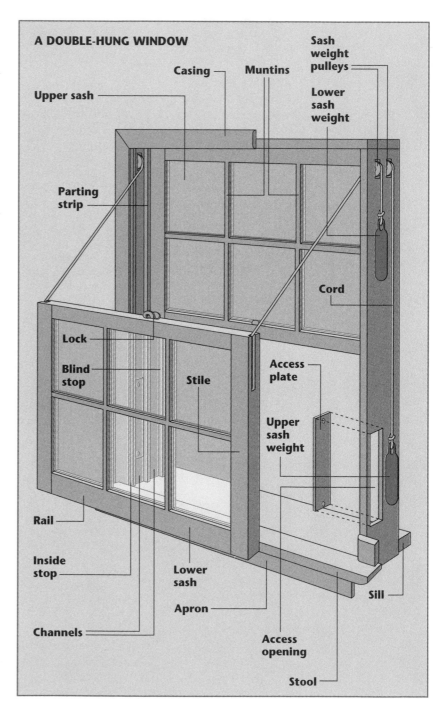

A DOUBLE-HUNG WINDOW

Casing · Muntins · Sash weight pulleys · Upper sash · Lower sash weight · Parting strip · Cord · Lock · Blind stop · Stile · Access plate · Upper sash weight · Rail · Inside stop · Lower sash · Apron · Sill · Channels · Access opening · Stool

Freeing a paint-bound sash

TOOLKIT
- Utility knife
- Putty knife
- Mallet
- Hammer

From outside:
- Prybar

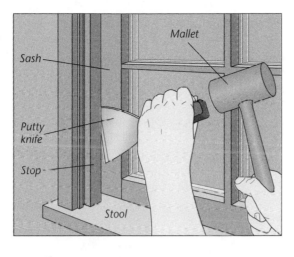

Moving the sash

There are three ways that you can move a paint-bound sash: Work a stiff putty knife between the sash and frame after you've scored the paint along the edges with a utility knife. Tap with a mallet to break the paint seal (*left*).

From outside, wedge a prybar between the sill and sash; work alternately at each end so the sash moves up evenly. Protect the sill with a wood block.

If the window is stuck open too wide to be pried, place a wood block on the sash at one side; tap with a hammer. Continue tapping, alternating sides, until the sash is freed.

Loosening a tight sash

TOOLKIT
- Butt chisel
- Hammer
- Screwdriver (optional)

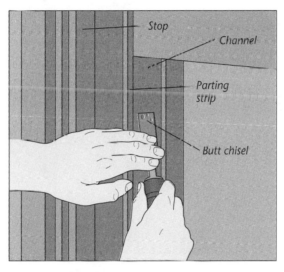

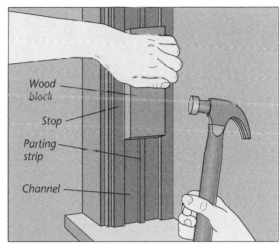

Cleaning the channels

Chisel off any dirt or large globs of paint (*above*); then sand the channels smooth. Coat all surfaces with paraffin so the sash moves easily.

Widening the channel

To widen the channel where stops are nailed, place a wood block wider than the channel at the point that binds. Tap the block against the stop until the sash moves (*above*).

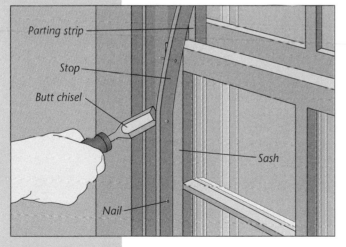

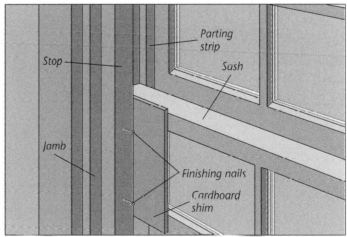

Repositioning the stops

First, pry off the stops and the nails holding them (*above, left*) after scoring the paint between the jambs and stops. Chisel any built-up paint off the edges of the sash, stops, and parting strip. Sand the edges smooth and apply paraffin. Nail the stops back on the jambs, using a thin cardboard shim between the stop and sash as a spacing guide (*above, right*); remove the shim.

Replacing sash weight cords with chains

TOOLKIT
- Slip-joint pliers
- Screwdriver
- Chisel

1 ▶ Removing the lower and upper sashes

Angle the lower sash out *(right)* after removing the inside stops *(page 89)*. Untie and slip each cord out of the groove (a nail keeps the cord from slipping through the pulley). Pull out each parting strip with slip-joint pliers *(below)*; use wood strips to protect the wood. Angle the upper sash out of the frame; remove the nail and disconnect the cords.

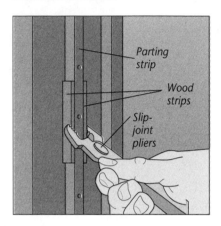

Parting strip
Wood strips
Slip-joint pliers

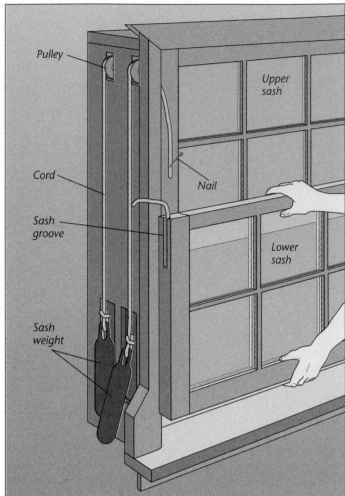

Pulley
Upper sash
Cord
Nail
Sash groove
Lower sash
Sash weight

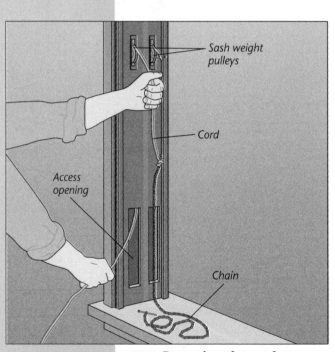

Sash weight pulleys
Cord
Access opening
Chain

2 Removing the cords

Remove the screws holding each access plate and pry off the plates with a chisel to get at the sash weights or, if there are no plates, pry off the window's casings. Tie an end of each new chain to an end of each cord; slip a nail through each chain's other end. Untie the weights; pull the cords out of the openings *(above, left)*.

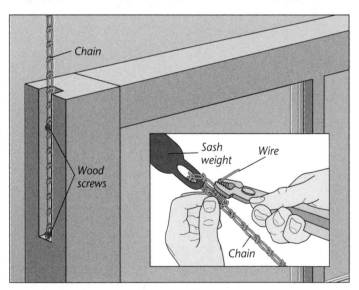

Chain
Wood screws
Sash weight
Wire
Chain

3 Attaching the chains

Loop each chain through the hole in each weight; using pliers, secure the chains with wire *(inset)*. Clear the access openings of debris and replace the weights. Adjust the chains so the weights will be 2" above the stool when the sash is up. Secure the chains to the sash channels with wood screws *(above, right)*; replace the upper sash, parting strips, access plates, bottom sash, and stops, in that order, checking the operation of each sash.

Replacing a window pane

TOOLKIT
- Butt chisel
- Propane torch (optional)
- Long-nose pliers
- Putty knife

1 ▶ Removing the broken glass

CAUTION: Wear work gloves and safety goggles when removing shards. Tape newspaper to the inside of the sash to catch any fragments. Pad glass with several layers of newspaper when you're transporting it and dispose of it immediately. After removing large shards, chisel out remaining bits of glass and putty *(right)*. Soak any hard putty with linseed oil or gently heat it with a propane torch. Remove glazier's points with long-nose pliers. Clean and sand the wood; coat with wood sealer.

Have glass cut to size at the store. Measure the width and height of the sash opening and subtract 1/8" from each dimension. Take several measurements to allow for the sash being out of square.

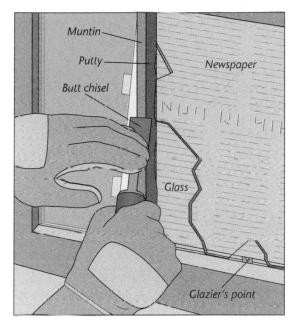

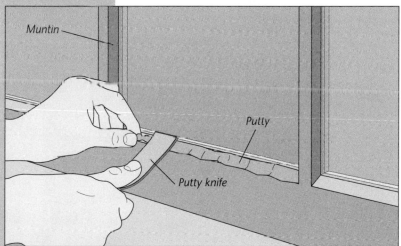

◀ 2 Applying putty

Working from outside the window, use a putty knife and your fingers to press a rope of glazing putty about 1/4" thick around the edges of the opening *(left)* to make a bed for the replacement glass.

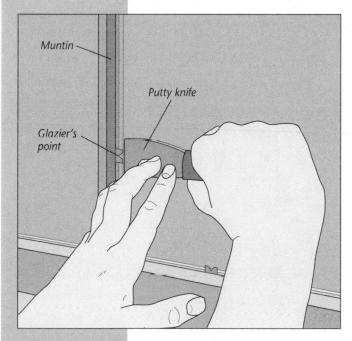

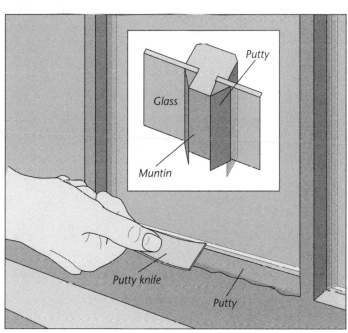

3 Installing the pane

Press the pane into place; remove excess putty. Push glazier's points into the frame with a putty knife *(above, left)*; use 2 points on each side for small panes and 1 point every 4" to 6" for larger ones. Roll more putty into a rope about 1/4" thick; apply it around the outside edges. With a putty knife, smooth and bevel the putty to form a neat seal *(above, right)*. When dry, paint to match the wood.

CASEMENT WINDOWS

A wooden or metal casement window has a sash hinged at the side and is operated either by a sliding rod (found in older windows) or by a crank and gear mechanism, as shown at right; the track for the extension arm is in the underside of the sash. A metal casement window seldom has problems if it's lubricated regularly with paraffin, light penetrating oil, or silicone spray.

If a window doesn't operate properly, check the gear assembly in the crank mechanism. Open the window partially and remove the screws that hold the operator to the frame. Pull the extension arm toward you along the track until it slips free, and through the window frame. If the gear teeth are worn, replace the unit with an exact duplicate. If dirt is the problem, clean the assembly with stiff wire or kerosene. Lubricate metal gears with powdered graphite, silicone spray, or petroleum jelly; turn the crank to spread the lubricant. Use silicone spray on nylon gears. If the gears still malfunction, replace the entire assembly with a duplicate.

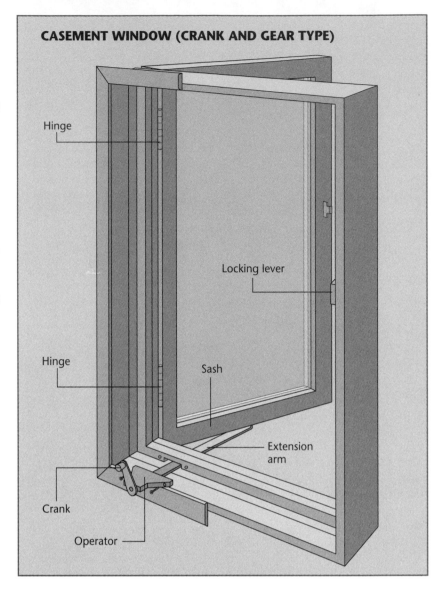

CASEMENT WINDOW (CRANK AND GEAR TYPE)

Hinge

Locking lever

Hinge

Sash

Extension arm

Crank

Operator

Repairing a pivot-mount rod

TOOLKIT
• Screwdriver

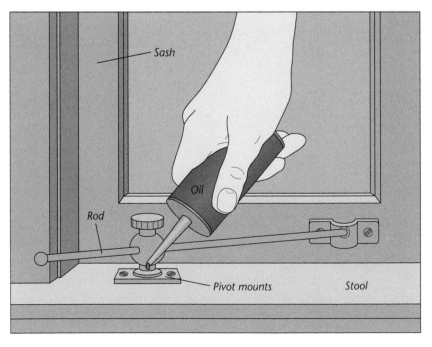

Sash

Oil

Rod

Pivot mounts

Stool

Cleaning and lubricating the parts
Look for hardened grease or globs of paint on the sliding rod. With steel wool, remove any dirt or paint from the rod; lubricate it with paraffin. Oil all pivot points *(left)* and tighten the screws holding the mounts to the sash and stool.

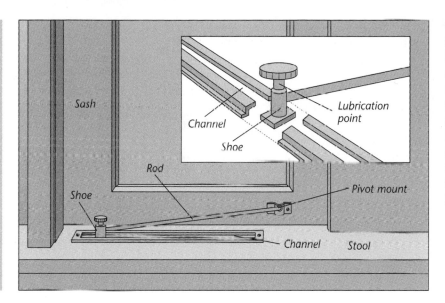

Repairing a sliding-shoe rod

TOOLKIT
• Screwdriver

Sash

Channel

Shoe

Rod

Shoe

Channel

Stool

Lubrication point

Pivot mount

Cleaning and lubricating the parts
If the mechanism is not working properly, unscrew the channel and clean both the channel and stool. Lubricate the channel *(inset)* with paraffin and replace it. Tighten all the screws and oil all the pivot points.

SLIDING WINDOWS

Sliding window sashes move along metal, wood, or vinyl tracks fitted into the window frame at the top and bottom *(below)*. To ease their movement, large sashes often have plastic rollers attached to the top and bottom, or to the bottom only.

The window can jam or not close properly if its catch is bent, loose, or damaged. For a paint-clogged sash, score the edges with a sharp utility knife, and then rock the sash from side to side to loosen it. Clean any dirt from the sides of the sash and the frame; lubricate both with paraffin. Use a wire brush to clean dirt from the track; for stubborn particles, use the blade of a screwdriver. Lubricate the track with paraffin to keep the sash movement smooth.

If the rollers are sticking, lubricate them with powdered graphite or silicone spray until they move freely. If they're broken, you'll need to remove the sash *(page 94)* and have a glazier replace the rollers.

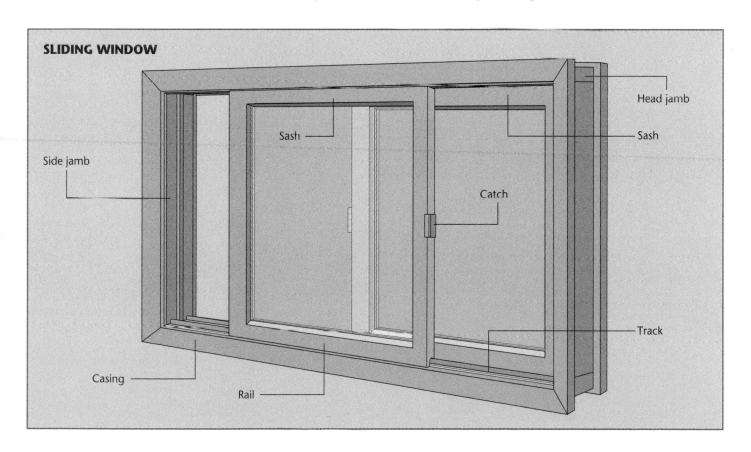

SLIDING WINDOW

Head jamb

Sash

Sash

Side jamb

Catch

Track

Casing

Rail

Reshaping a catch

Sliding windows are secured with a variety of catches; the type used depends on the manufacturer and whether the windows are made from metal or wood.

If the catch doesn't work properly, you may need to remove the sash from the frame to fix it. However, you may be able to reshape a bent catch. First, determine how much reshaping it will need to bring it flush with the widest diameter of the rail; then unscrew the catch from its position alongside the rail and clamp it in a vise. Using slip-joint pliers or a hammer, bend the catch to the proper angle. Replace it and check the latch operation—it should click as the window closes, and it should have to be depressed fully for the window to open. Replace a defective catch or one that is worn or broken with an exact duplicate.

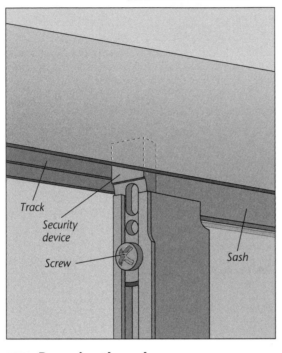

1 **Removing the sash**
To remove the sash, first look for any security devices at the top; loosen the screws holding them in place and remove the devices *(above, left)*.

Carefully lift the sash up to clear the track and angle the bottom edge out of the frame *(above, right)*. Align the top rollers with the key notches, if any.

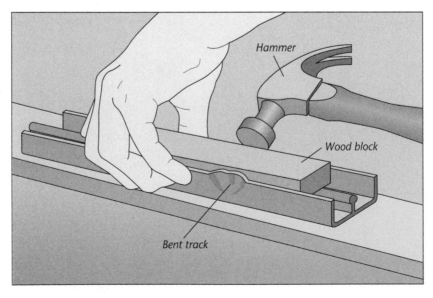

2 **Fixing the track**
Place a wood block in the track; using a hammer, tap the block against the bent metal until the side of the track is flat *(left)*. Replace the sash.

HOME REPAIR GLOSSARY

Batten
A thin strip of lumber used to seal vertical siding, or as a base for fastening some types of roofing.

Bonding agent
A glue-like product that bonds a concrete patch to the old concrete.

Caulk
Material used to create a watertight seal, such as between a bathtub and wall.

Cement, portland
A manufactured product, as opposed to natural cement. A basic ingredient in both mortar and concrete. Portland cement ingredients include lime, silica, alumina, and iron.

Circuit
Two or more wires providing a path for electric current to flow from the source through some device using electricity (such as a light) and back to the source.

Cleanout
An opening providing access to a drainline or trap; closed with a threaded plug.

Counterboring
Drilling a hole in advance of setting in a screw at a depth that leaves the head of the screw below the surface of the wood. Allows for the hole to be plugged, concealing the screw head.

Countersinking
Drilling a hole in wood to allow a flathead screw to sit flush with the surface.

Curing
Ensuring that cement-based products such as mortar, stucco patching compound, or concrete patching compound harden properly; this is done by keeping the patch moist for several days.

Dry rot
Rot in lumber caused by a fungus, which reduces the wood to powder.

Fascia
Boards attached to rafter ends at the eaves and along gables.

Feathering
A method of spreading and smoothing edges of a material, such as joint compound patches on wallboard.

Flange
A rim that attaches one object to another, such as the part of aluminum or vinyl siding which interlocks with other panels.

Flashing
Material that seals a roof or wall at its vulnerable points, such as at valley and eaves and against chimneys.

Furring strip
Thin strip of wood attached to the structure to provide a nailing base for siding, or for ceiling or wall materials.

Gasket
Device (usually rubber) used to make a joint between two parts watertight. Term is sometimes used interchangeably with washer.

Grout
A thin cement-based material used to seal the joints between ceramic tiles.

Jamb
A board that forms the top or side of a frame surrounding a window or door.

Joint compound
Filler for joints between sheets of gypsum wallboard.

Lath
A material, usually wood strips or metal, to which plaster is applied.

Lime, hydrated
An ingredient in mortar; increases its workability.

Locknut
Nut used to secure a part, such as a toilet inlet valve, in place.

Mastic
A type of adhesive used for ceramic tile.

Mortar
Material used as a base and to bond masonry units, such as brick and stone, together. Typically composed of water, hydrated lime, portland cement, and sand.

Mortise
A recess cut in a piece of wood, such as for a hinge or strike plate.

O-ring
Narrow rubber ring; used in some faucets as packing to prevent leaking around the stem and in some faucets to prevent leaking at the base of the spout.

Packing
Material that stops leaking around the handle of a faucet or valve.

Penetrating oil
A common household lubricant for metal parts such as door hinges. Also used to loosen threaded plumbing joints where corrosion has fused the parts together.

Pilot hole
A hole drilled into a piece of wood for a nail or screw to follow; guides the fastener and prevents splitting. It is slightly smaller than the shaft of the nail or the threads of the screw.

Plaster
A material used for walls and ceilings composed of lime, sand, and water.

Priming
Applying a preparatory product to a surface prior to painting.

Rail
Horizontal member of a door structure, along the top, bottom, and sometimes middle of the door.

Receptacle
Outlet, usually on a wall, into which an electrical device is plugged.

Resilient flooring
Flexible sheet or tile flooring; can be made of a number of materials including vinyl, cork, and rubber.

Sash
The part of a window holding the glass.

Screw terminal
Threaded screw found on sockets, switches, and receptacles; used to make wire connections.

Seat
Part of a valve, such as in a compression faucet, onto which the washer fits to cut off the flow of water.

Sheathing
The exterior skin of a house under the siding, typically plywood or exterior gypsum board.

Shim
Small piece of metal or other rigid material used to adjust alignment, such as of a hinge or strike plate.

Shoe molding
Covers the joint between the tread and the riser on a staircase.

Silicone grease
A type of synthetic grease used to lubricate faucet parts; non-petroleum base won't break down rubber parts.

Sleeper
A board fastened to a concrete floor to provide a nailing surface for flooring materials.

Soffit
The area below the eaves, where the roof overhangs the exterior walls.

Stile
Vertical member of a door structure.

Stop
A vertical piece of wood attached to a window or door frame that the window or door butts against.

Strike plate
A metal plate on a door jamb into which the latch assembly fits when the door is closed.

Striking
The act of compacting and shaping a mortar joint with a trowel or joint-striking tool.

Subfloor
Material such as plywood that forms a base for flooring materials. (An underlayment is generally applied between the subfloor and the flooring.)

Toenailing
The act of driving a nail at an angle from one piece into another.

Tooling
Another term for striking mortar joints.

Trap
Device (most often a curved section of pipe) that holds a water seal to prevent sewer gases from escaping into a home through a fixture drain.

Undercutting
A procedure where old but intact material is removed from the inner side of holes or large cracks at an angle; ensures that patching material will form a strong bond with the solid material around the hole.

Underlayment
A layer between the subfloor and finish flooring. Asphalt building paper is commonly used for wood floors; plywood is used for ceramic tile or resilient flooring.

Underwriters' knot
A type of knot used to tie wires in electric cords to relieve strain on screw terminal connections.

Wallboard, gypsum
A panel made with a core of gypsum rock, which covers interior walls and ceilings.

Weather stripping
Material applied to door and window bottom and jambs to seal against drafts and moisture.

Wet sanding
A method of sanding joint compound for wallboard. The compound is dampened with a sponge, and then the area is sanded with a sanding block and wet-or-dry sandpaper.

INDEX